Age of dinosaurs.
Dinosaurs are at
their peak in size,
variety and numbers
and dominate every
continent.

'K-T extinction'.
End of the
dinosaurs.

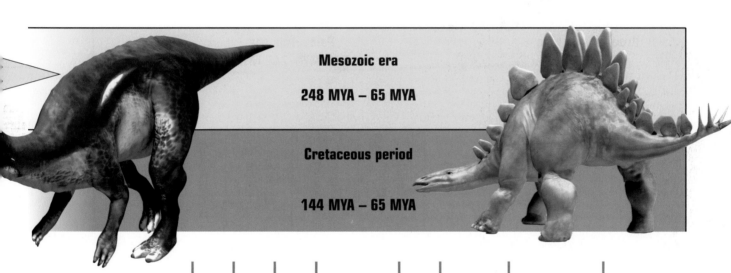

Mesozoic era

248 MYA – 65 MYA

Cretaceous period

144 MYA – 65 MYA

Hadrosaurus
Velociraptor
Protoceratops   Centrosaurus
                 Troodon
Giganotosaurus   Tyrannosaurus
Spinosaurus   Triceratops
                 Ankylosaurus
Argentinosaurus Edmontosaurus
Nodosaurus

Deinonychus

Acrocanthosaurus

Iguanadon

Baryonyx

3

FULL TIMELINE

Oceans and atmosphere form. Earliest life forms in oceans.

Trilobites dominate seas. Still no land life.

Earliest land plants appear.

Insects flourish. First reptiles evolve. Shrubs, ferns and trees dominate land.

Massive volcanic eruptions cause mass extinctions, wiping out 90% of marine life and 70% of land life!

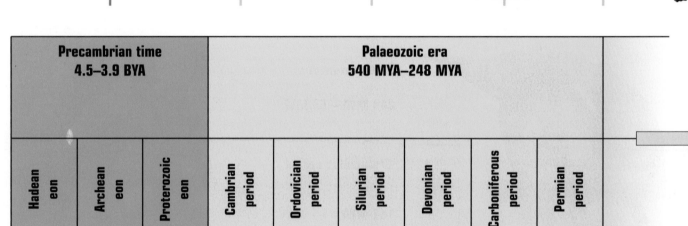

Precambrian time 4.5–3.9 BYA			Palaeozoic era 540 MYA–248 MYA					
Hadean eon	Archean eon	Proterozoic eon	Cambrian period	Ordovician period	Silurian period	Devonian period	Carboniferous period	Permian period

The Earth forms!

Sea plants begin photosynthesis.

First fish evolve.

Fish dominate oceans. Spiders and mites are first land creatures. First amphibians evolve. First forests form.

Synapsids, such as Dimetrodon and amphibians such as Eryops dominate land.

4

'K-T extinction'
End of the
dinosaurs.

Dinosaurs
dominate.
First mammals
evolve.

Mammals such
as horses, bats
and whales
evolve.

Most modern
birds and
mammals have
evolved.

'Great Ice Age'
Neanderthals and
Homo sapiens, or modern
humans, evolve.
Smilodon (saber-toothed
tiger), mastodons and
mammoths evolve.

Mesozoic era 248 MYA–65 MYA			Cenozoic era 65 MYA–NOW							
			Tertiary period (65 MYA – 1.8MYA)						Quaternary period (1.8MYA – NOW)	
Triassic period	Jurassic period	Cretaceous period	Paleocene epoch	Eocene epoch	Oligocene epoch	Miocene epoch	Pliocene epoch		Pleistocene epoch	Holocene epoch

Sauropsids
such as the
archosaurs
dominate.
First cynodonts
such as
Cynognathus
evolve.
Marine reptiles
evolve.

**Age of
dinosaurs.
Dinosaurs are
at their peak in
size, variety and
numbers and
dominate every
continent.**

Mammals
dominate.
Early carnivores
evolve.

Creodonts
evolve.
Modern
mammals
become
dominant.

Hominids, the
ape-like
ancestors of
humans evolve.
Thylacosmilus
and other early
saber-tooths
evolve.

Last ice
age ends.
Human
civilization
develops.

EVOLUTION

The Earth, and all life on it, is constantly changing. Life had been on Earth for at least 3,260 million years before the dinosaurs appeared. The Palaeozoic era was from 540 to 250 million years ago, and was known as 'the age of ancient life'.

By 245–235 million years ago (the Mesozoic era) a large number of reptiles roamed the earth. Some of these were dinosaurs, including herbivorous rhynchosaurs and carnivorous archosaurs.

Dinosaurs appeared about 230 million years ago, during the Triassic period. Their evolution spread over the Jurassic and Cretaceaous periods, a total of 165 million years.

Dinosaurs completely dominated the land in a way that no other group of animals had done. Eight hundred species have been identified so far. No one knows where they came from.

Extinction

About 65 million years ago (the end of the Cretaceous period), 70 per cent of living species, including the dinosaurs and flying reptiles suddenly became extinct. Crocodiles and many other reptiles survived.

Tsunami breaking wave

Dimetrodon

Archaeopteryx

Crocodile

The most popular explanation for this extinction is that an asteroid from space hit earth. There has been evidence of an enormous meteorite colliding with the Earth 65 million years ago. The meteorite may have been a single asteroid, bits from asteroid collisions, or debris from a comet. This would probably have thrown up an enormous amount of dust into the atmosphere which would have blocked out the sun and made the whole world dark for several months.

It might also have caused other natural disasters such as tsunamis and earthquakes. All plant life would have died, therefore plant eaters would not have been able to survive. In turn, carnivores would have had no food, causing them to die.

Other theories include a period of intense volcanic activity which may have caused changes such as global warming and effects on plant life. Another argument is that a drastic drop in sea level would have made the climate more extreme. It is difficult to imagine how this could have had such an effect. A third theory is that the climate changed enough to make earth too cold or hot for reptilian life, but this does not explain how some reptiles, such as crocodiles, survived.

The Cenozoic era began 65 million years ago and is often called the 'age of mammals', because mammals thrived at this time.

Scientists believe that birds are descendants of the dinosaurs. They may have come from small meat eaters. You can see the similarity, especially when you compare the skeleton of dinosaurs to the skeleton of the oldest known bird, Archaeopteryx, which lived about 140 million years ago.

BRACHIOSAURUS

Tree-top grazing giant

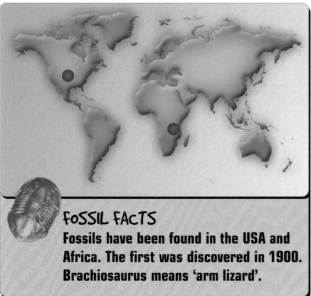

FOSSIL FACTS
Fossils have been found in the USA and Africa. The first was discovered in 1900. Brachiosaurus means 'arm lizard'.

Brachiosaurus was named in 1903 and gets its name from its long front limbs. It was 82 ft long and 49 ft high.

For many years it was thought to be the world's biggest dinosaur, but recent discoveries – such as Argentinosaurus – were proved to be bigger in terms of sheer mass.

Appearance and diet

Brachiosaurus walked on four legs, had a long neck, tiny head and a comparatively short, thick tail. It had chisel-like teeth to nip leaves and fruit from the trees. It had nostrils on top of its head, which meant it could eat almost constantly without interfering with its breathing. It swallowed its food whole, without chewing.

To help with its digestion, brachiosaurus swallowed stones. These stayed in its gizzard. Tough leaves and plant fibers would be ground up by the stones as they went through.

Circulation system

To pump blood all the way up its long neck to its tiny brain, Brachiosaurus had to have a powerful heart and broad, strong blood vessels, with valves to prevent the blood obeying gravity and flowing backwards. Scientists once thought Brachiosaurus actually had two brains, the second near the hip area – but current thinking is that this was simply an enlargement in the spinal cord.

Habitat

At first, scientists believed it must have been an aquatic dinosaur, spending all its time in the water and using its long neck and the nostrils on top of its head as a kind of snorkel for breathing. However, studies showed that water pressure would have stopped Brachiosaurus from breathing properly when submerged.

Dinosaur Data

PRONUNCIATION:	BRACK-EE-OH-**SAWR**-US
SUBORDER:	SAUROPODOMORPHA
FAMILY:	BRACHIOSAURIDAE
DESCRIPTION:	LONG-NECKED **HERBIVORE**
FEATURES:	HUGE FRONT LIMBS; TINY HEAD
DIET:	HERBIVORE

MEGA FACTS

- **Brachiosaurus may well have lived to be 100 years old.**

- **It probably traveled in herds.**

- **Brachiosaurus needed to consume 440 lb of food *every day* to fuel its massive body.**

- **It weighed 20 times as much as a large elephant!**

- **A full-size replica of a Brachiosaurus skeleton is mounted in O'Hare International Airport, Chicago.**

Scientists now believe that Brachiosaurus lived completely on land. Although their fossilized footprints have been found beside shorelines (they probably went there to drink) they have also been found in areas that 156–145 million years ago would have had very little water.

In 2003, a computer simulation run by Dr Donald Henderson in Canada, showed that Brachiosaurus would have floated rather than sunk if it had fallen into deep water – its hollow backbones would have helped it to float, though it would probably have rolled onto its sides in the water rather than staying upright.

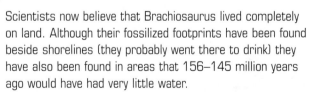

ARGENTINOSAURUS

Gigantic long-necked herbivore

FOSSIL FACTS
The only fossils were found in Argentina in 1988.

Argentinosaurus means 'lizard from Argentina'. It was named in 1993 by palaeontologists José F. Bonaparte and Rodolfo Coria after the country where it was found.

Appearance

Argentinosaurus may have grown up to 130 ft long, 69 ft tall and about 30 ft wide and weighed 90–110 tons.

An entire skeleton has yet to be discovered. Only about 10% of the Argentinosaurus skeleton was found, and nothing at all from its neck or tail. Scientists used the bones that *were* found to work out which other dinosaurs Argentinosaurus was related to. They then made their 'best guesses' at its appearance based on what those other dinosaurs looked like.

It would have looked very similar to a Brachiosaurus with a long tail, and a tiny triangular-shaped head on the end of its long neck. It would have needed a big, powerful heart to pump blood all the way up that long neck to its tiny brain.

Backbone

Scientists think its backbone worked in a special way to support the vast weight of the animal. The backbones interlinked to make the whole back into a sort of bridge of bone.

Dinosaur Data

PRONUNCIATION:	AHY-GEN-**TEEN**-OH-**SAWR**-US
SUBORDER:	SAUROPODOMORPHA
FAMILY:	TITANOSAURIA
DESCRIPTION:	GIGANTIC LONG-NECKED HERBIVORE
FEATURES:	SPECIAL INTERLOCKING BACKBONE, LONG NECK
DIET:	MOSTLY CONIFERS, ALSO FLOWERS, FRUIT AND SEEDS

Curiously for such a big animal, the bones were hollow – perhaps they evolved that way to reduce weight and let Argentinosaurus move its vast bulk around more quickly.

Diet

Argentinosaurus was a herbivore, living on plants. It would have had to eat a huge amount to keep its massive body going, and probably spent most of its waking moments eating. Luckily, the area where it lived was full of lush vegetation. This is the area we now call Patagonia. It would have eaten mostly conifers, seeds, fruit and flowering plants.

The biggest animal ever to live is a modern day giant, the Blue Whale. Argentinosaurus *was* the biggest animal that ever lived on land, though. Its relative, Seismosaurus was actually longer, but less tall, wide and heavy.

Argentinosaurus reigns supreme – at least until the next 'big' discovery!

MEGA FACTS

- A single vertebra (backbone) from Argentinosaurus is taller than a child and measures 5 ft across!

- Argentinosaurus was preyed on by the massive meat eater Giganotosaurus and perhaps an even larger recently-discovered meat eater – *Mapusaurus Roseae*, that hunted in packs!

- Thanks to its long neck, Argentinosaurus would have no trouble looking in at a third or fourth storey window.

- In its 'teenage' years when it was growing fastest, Argentinosaurus could gain about 100 lb a day!

- Argentinosaurus was as long as four buses!

DIPLODOCUS

Gigantic long-necked herbivore

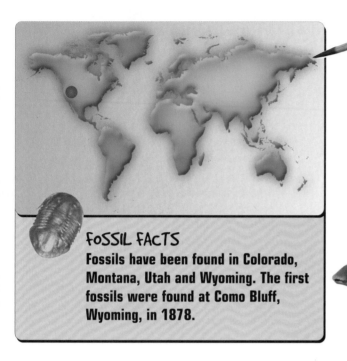

FOSSIL FACTS
Fossils have been found in Colorado, Montana, Utah and Wyoming. The first fossils were found at Como Bluff, Wyoming, in 1878.

Diplodocus means 'double beamed lizard'. It was named in 1878, by Othniel Charles Marsh. The name comes from an unusual feature of the bones in the middle of its tail, where twin extensions of protruding bone run backward and forward. They would have protected blood vessels in the tail if it dragged on the floor, or if the dinosaur pressed its tail against the floor to help balance while rearing on its back legs.

Diplodocus skeleton

Permian period	**Triassic period**	**Jurassic period**	**Cretaceous period**
90-248 million years ago)	(248-176 million years ago)	(176-130 million years ago)	(130-66 million years ago)

Appearance

Diplodocus was one of the longest land animals that ever lived. At 89 ft long it was a true giant. It stood around 20 ft high at the hip and weighed 10–11 tons. Diplodocus had hollow bones and so it weighed only an eighth of the similar-sized Brachiosaurus.

Much of its length was accounted for by its long neck and even longer whip-like tail. Its head was tiny, with an elongated snout and nostril on the top of the skull.

In 1990, a new Diplodocus skeleton was found with skin impressions. This suggests diplodocus had row of spines down its back.

MEGA FACTS

- The life-sized replica of diplodocus, named 'Dippy', stands outside the Carnegie Museum of Natural History in Pittsburgh.

- Some scientists believe Diplodocus could swing its long tail as a weapon. If so, the speed at the very tip of the tail would have broken the sound barrier!

Brain

Diplodocus had a brain the size of a fist. It was once thought that Diplodocus had two brains, one in the skull and one close to the base of the spine. Actually, this second 'brain' was simply a concentration of nerves that helped to control the back legs and tail.

Scientists believe Diplodocus could not lift its head very far from the ground. The longer neck may have allowed Diplodocus to push its neck and head a good distance into overgrown forest areas to find food. It could also swing the neck from side to side, allowing it to graze on a wide area without actually moving. Scientists think that Diplodocus would have spent almost every waking moment eating, just to keep its massive body going.

It was a quadruped. Each pillar-like leg had five toes, and one toe on each foot had a thumb claw, which might have been used for self-defense.

Diet

Diplodocus was a herbivore. Its main food would have been conifer leaves and ferns. Its simple, peg-like teeth could strip soft foliage like ferns but couldn't chew them up. Diplodocus swallowed small stones (called gastroliths) to help grind up its food in its stomach.

Dinosaur Data

PRONUNCIATION:	DIP-**LOD**-OH-KUS
SUBORDER:	SAUROPODOMORPHA
FAMILY:	DILODOCIDAE
DESCRIPTION:	LONG-NECKED HERBIVORE
FEATURES:	LONG NECK, WHIPLASH TAIL, HOLLOW BONES, TINY HEAD
DIET:	FERNS AND CONIFERS

APATOSAURUS

Formerly known as Brontosaurus

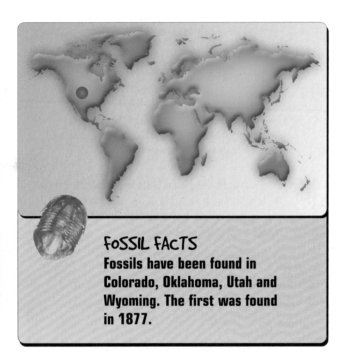

FOSSIL FACTS
Fossils have been found in Colorado, Oklahoma, Utah and Wyoming. The first was found in 1877.

Apatosaurus means 'deceptive lizard'. In 1877, American palaeontologist Othniel C. Marsh described and named a dinosaur called Apatosaurus. In 1879, he described and named another set of dinosaur remains, and – believing them to be from a different creature – christened them Brontosaurus.

Appearance

In 1903, it was discovered that Brontosaurus was in fact simply a fully-grown Apatosaurus! However, the name Brontosaurus was not officially removed from lists until 1974, and it is still popular with many people.

Apatosaurus was some 69–90 ft long, 10–15 ft tall at the hip and weighed 27 tons. Its head was tiny at only 2 ft in length. Its long neck had 15 vertebrae, and a long, whip-like tail which accounted for 50 ft of its whole length. In the front part of its jaw were peg-like teeth, ideal for stripping leaves and browsing on vegetation. Apatosaurus would have had to eat almost constantly when awake – fortunately, nostrils placed on the top of the skull meant it could eat and breathe at the same time.

Apatosaurus swallowed its food without chewing it, and to help with its digestion, it swallowed stones which stayed in its gizzard. Stones swallowed for this purpose are called gastroliths.

A study in 1999 used computer modeling to test the mobility of the neck of Apatosaurus. The results showed that they could not have lifted their heads any higher than 10–13 ft (just a little higher than their backs), and must most of the time have held their heads downwards or straight out. (They could move their heads freely from side to side, though.)

Dinosaur Data

PRONUNCIATION:	A-**PAT**-OH-**SAWR**-US
SUBORDER:	SAUROPODA
FAMILY:	DIPLODOCIDAE
DESCRIPTION:	LARGE, SLOW-MOVING HERBIVORE
FEATURES:	THICK LEGS, TINY HEAD, LONG NECK, LONG THIN TAIL
DIET:	HERBIVORE: LEAVES, PLANTS, MOSSES

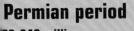

Permian period	Triassic period	Jurassic period	Cretaceous period
90-248 million years ago)	(248-176 million years ago)	(176-130 million years ago)	(130-66 million years ago)

The biggest predator around at the time, Allosaurus, was only 15 ft tall – an Apatosaurus whose head was raised even by this limited amount would place its head 18 ft off the ground, making it almost impossible for the carnivore to attack its head and neck.

Like other sauropods, Apatosaurus young hatched from huge eggs. It is assumed that Apatosaurus laid their eggs as they walked, and did not take care of their eggs.

MEGA FACTS

- Brain the size of a large apple.

- In the 1933 film *King Kong*, an Apatosaurus was depicted as a bloodthirsty carnivore – quite unlike the gentle plant-eating giant it really was.

- Apatosaurus had thick skin to protect it. Just as well – one of its vertebrae was found with Allosaurus tooth marks in it!

- Fossilized Apatosaurus footprints have been found that measured more than a yard across!

Apatosaurus

Apatosaurus skeleton

15

SEISMOSAURUS

Giant whip-tailed herbivore

P
L
A
N
T

E
A
T
E
R
S

Seismosaurus means 'earthquake lizard' or 'earth shaker lizard', named because a creature of its fantastic size must have surely shaken the Earth as it walked. It was discovered in 1979, and described and named by David D. Gillette in 1991. Because of its huge size, and the rocks in which it was found, it took 13 years to excavate.

Seismosaurus is currently thought to be the longest animal that ever lived. Its length was estimated originally at around 170 ft – in 2004, this was revised to 110 ft. This still leaves Seismosaurus at the top of the 'longest dinosaur' list, and just ahead of the previous longest-ever animal, the blue whale (100 ft). It probably weighed nearly 45 tons.

All our information about Seismosaurus comes from the fossilized bones from the hip and part of the back, which were found in 1979. Found mingled with the fossilized bones were the fossilized remains of more than 200 'gastroliths' – small stones that Seismosaurus swallowed to help it digest its food. It is possible that the death of this specimen was caused when it swallowed a particularly large stone, which stuck in its throat and blocked its airway.

Seismosaurus hallorum

Seismosaurus

FOSSIL FACTS
Fossils have been found only in New Mexico.

Appearance

Seismosaurus would have looked very like a large Diplodocus, and may not have been much taller, as it had short legs compared to its body length. It had four pillar-like legs with five-toed feet like an elephant, a long neck, and a long, thin tail to counterbalance neck and head. Its head was tiny compared to its length, and housed a very small brain.

Permian period	Triassic period	Jurassic period	Cretaceous period
0-248 million years ago)	(248-176 million years ago)	(176-130 million years ago)	(130-66 million years ago)

MEGA FACTS

- Probably hatched from eggs like other sauropods.

- Seismosaurus may have lived to be 100 years old.

- Seismosaurus remains are so similar to those of Diplodocus, some scientists think Seismosaurus may not be a separate type of dinosaur at all, but a big new version of Diplodocus.

It had peg-like teeth in the front part of its mouth, ideally suited for stripping the leaves from trees and grazing on plants. It had nostrils on the top of its skull, which allowed it to eat and breathe at the same time. It may have used the whip-like tail for protection.

Seismosaurus' long neck would have usually been held parallel to the ground. It might have allowed the creature to poke its head into dense forest areas to reach leaves otherwise inaccessible to the bulky dinosaurs, or maybe to eat soft pterodophytes that grew in wet areas too swampy to enter safely. Its main diet item was probably conifers, huge forests of which flourished in its time.

Dinosaur Data

PRONUNCIATION:	SIZE-MOH-**SAWR**-US
SUBORDER:	SAUROPODOMORPHA
FAMILY:	DIPLODOCIDAE
DESCRIPTION:	INCREDIBLY LONG HERBIVORE
FEATURES:	LONG NECK, TINY HEAD, WHIP-LIKE TAIL
DIET:	LEAVES, FERNS, MOSSES

HADROSAURUS

Duck-billed browsing herbivore

PLANT EATERS

fOSSIL FACTS
Fossils have been found along the coast of New Jersey. The first was found at Haddonfield, New Jersey in 1858, by William Parker Foulke.

Appearance and diet

Hadrosaurus was a herbivore that browsed along the shrub lands and marshes of the Atlantic coast of America 84–71 million years ago. It had a bulky body, stiff tail, and hoof-like nails on its four feet. It was a good swimmer, and may have ventured substantial distances from shore; it could also have spent time in the warm waters. It grew to between 23–30 ft in length, and 10–13 ft high – taller than a house if it stood on its back legs! It weighed 4,000 lb.

Hadrosaurus means 'heavy lizard'. It was studied and named by palaeontologist Joseph Leidy in 1858.

When Hadrosaurus was discovered, it was the most complete dinosaur skeleton that had been found. During the 1800s, various specimens of fossilized bones unlike those of any living animal, and much, much bigger, had been found in Europe and North America.

In 1841, Dr Richard Owen, a British authority on anatomy, suggested these bones belonged to a group of large reptiles, all of which had completely died out long ago. It was he who first coined the name 'dinosaurs', meaning 'terrible lizards'. Until Hadrosaurus came along, though, no one was able to say what one of these 'dinosaurs' would have looked like.

The remains dug up in 1858 included, for the first time, enough of a dinosaur's skeleton to document its anatomy. It was also the first dinosaur fossil ever mounted and put on display in a museum. The study of dinosaurs became a well-respected science.

Hadrosaurus

Statue of Hadrosaurus

MEGA FACTS

- Even though Hadrosuarus had a whole dinosaur family named after it, no Hadrosaurus skull has ever been discovered. The shape of its head is deduced from the skulls of other duck-billed dinosaurs.

- In October 2003, a life-size statue of Hadrosaurus, cast in bronze, was unveiled in Haddonfield, close to the place the first Hadrosaurus was found.

- State Official – in 1991, Hadrosaurus became the official 'state dinosaur' of New Jersey.

Its back legs were longer than its front legs, and this at first led scientists to believe it spent most of its time on its hind legs, in a kind of 'kangaroo-like' stance. We now know that it spent most of its time on all fours. The most recent evidence suggests that Hadrosaurus held its whole rear body aloft, to balance it as it leaned its upper body forward in movements similar to those of modern birds. The front limbs would have been used for foraging.

Dinosaur Data

PRONUNCIATION:	**HAD**-ROW-**SAWR**-US
SUBORDER:	ORNITOPODA
FAMILY:	HADROSAURIDAE
DESCRIPTION:	MASSIVE DUCK-BILLED HERBIVORE
FEATURES:	BULKY BODY, TOOTHLESS BEAK
DIET:	LEAVES, TWIGS

MELANOROSAURUS

Giant herbivorous dinosaur

FOSSIL FACTS
Fossils were found in South Africa in 1924 by Sydney H. Haugh.

Melanorosaurus

Melanorosaurus means 'Black Mountain lizard' and comes from the Greek words *melanos* (black), *oros* (mountain) and *sauros* (lizard). It was named by the British palaeontologist Sydney H. Haugh in 1924 after the Thaba Nyama or Black Mountain in South Africa where the fossil was found.

Appearance

Melanorosaurus lived in the early Triassic period. At 39 ft long, 14 ft tall and probably weighing around 5,000 lb, it was the largest land animal of its time.

Like all sauropods, Melanorosaurus was herbivorous and had a bulky body, long neck and tail, a relatively small skull and brain and erect limbs reminiscent of the limbs of elephants. For some time it was believed that Melanorosaurus was a quadruped, as were many of the giant sauropods.

However, recently scientists have speculated that the sturdy hind limbs with their strong, dense bones could have enabled the creature to walk on its two hind legs, a theory that is given extra weight by the fact that the fore limbs were rather shorter than the hind limbs.

This ability to walk on two legs would make it a facultative biped, a creature that *could* walk on two legs but didn't have to – it may well have taken advantage of this ability to rear up on its hind legs in its quest for tasty leaves!

MEGA FACTS

- Biggest dinosaur of the Triassic era! At 39 ft long, Melanorosaurus was the largest dinosaur of its day — only in the Cretaceous period and later have larger dinosaurs been found.

- So far no Melanorosaurus skull has been discovered. However it is believed that its skull would have been very similar in shape to those of the other giant sauropods, many of whose skulls have been found.

- Whilst its limbs had dense bones, its spinal bones and vertebrae had hollows to reduce their weight.

Diet

Melanorosaurus' diet would have consisted of branches, leaves and twigs, with its height and long neck allowing it to easily reach the tops of trees. Taking large mouthfuls of food at a time, it would use its serrated leaf-shaped teeth to snap off branches and then chew the vegetation quite effectively before swallowing. Its long neck meant it could browse over a sizeable area by just moving its head and neck, this allowed it to reduce the amount of energy it would have to use up in moving — important when considering how much energy from plants it would take to maintain such a large body.

Dinosaur Data

PRONUNCIATION:	MEL-UH-**NOR**-UH-**SAWR**-US
SUBORDER:	SAUROPODOMORPHA
FAMILY:	MELANOROSAURIDAE
DESCRIPTION:	GIANT LONG-NECKED **HERBIVORE**
FEATURES:	LONG NECK AND TAIL, BULKY BODY, LEAF-SHAPED SERRATED TEETH
DIET:	BRANCHES, LEAVES AND TWIGS

SALTASAURUS

Armor-plated herbivore

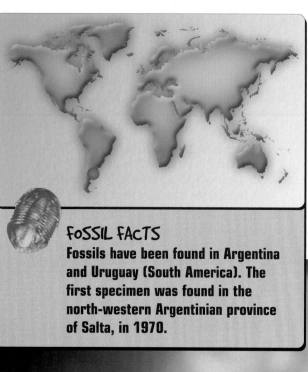

Dinosaur Data

PRONUNCIATION:	SALT-AH-**SAWR**-US
SUBORDER:	SAUROPODOMORPHA
FAMILY:	TITANOSAURIDAE
DESCRIPTION:	ARMORED SAUROPOD
FEATURES:	BONY ARMOR PLATES ON BACK AND SIDES
DIET:	LOW-GROWING FERNS, LEAVES

FOSSIL FACTS

Fossils have been found in Argentina and Uruguay (South America). The first specimen was found in the north-western Argentinian province of Salta, in 1970.

Permian period	Triassic period	Jurassic period	Cretaceous period
90-248 million years ago)	(248-176 million years ago)	(176-130 million years ago)	(130-66 million years ago)

Saltasaurus means 'lizard from Salta'. It is named after the Argentinian province of Salta where it was found by José Bonaparte and Jaime Powell in 1980.

Appearance

Saltsaurus was a sauropod, 40 ft long and weighed 7 tons. It had a bulky body, four stout legs ending in five-toed feet, a long neck ending in a tiny head, and a stout tail that tapered to whiplash thinness.

Its neck was shorter than that of most sauropods, but would still have helped it to feed on vegetation out of the reach of shorter herbivores. It had blunt teeth, in the back part of its mouth only. Some scientists believe it could rear up on its hind legs for short periods of time, perhaps using its tail for extra support and balance.

Saltasaurus lived about 70–65 million years ago. In most parts of the world at this time, sauropod dinosaurs were giving way to the more successful duck-billed dinosaurs.

South America, though, was an island continent and life evolved there somewhat differently. The duckbills never made much of an impression there, and sauropods continued to evolve there long after they had largely died out elsewhere.

MEGA FACTS

- A large nesting ground discovered in 1997 may have belonged to Saltasaurus. Remains showed that several hundred holes and been dug and eggs about 4–5 in. in diameter laid in them. The nests were then buried under dirt and vegetation to conceal them from predators.

- Communal nest building shows that Saltasaurus probably lived and traveled in herds.

- Saltasaurus eggs had a shell ¼ in. thick.

Armor plating

This may explain the most distinctive feature of Saltasaurus – unlike any previously-found sauropods, it had armor plating! Its back and sides were covered in circular and oval bony plates, up to 5 in. in diameter. It is thought horns or spikes may have stuck out from these plates, but firm evidence for this is yet to be found.

The discovery of Saltasaurus completely changed the way scientists thought about the sauropods. It had been assumed until then that the sauropods' size alone was enough to protect them from predators – so when Titanosaurus remains were found with armor plates, it had been reclassified as an ankylosaur. Saltasaurus showed that a dinosaur could have armour *and* still be a sauropod, and Titanosaurus was returned to the sauropod fold.

TITANOSAURUS

Giant armored herbivore

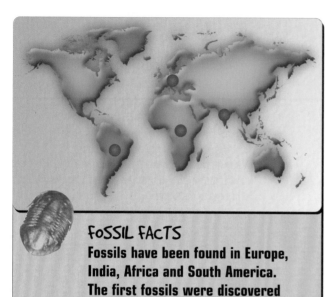

FOSSIL FACTS
Fossils have been found in Europe, India, Africa and South America. The first fossils were discovered in India.

Titanosaurus means 'titanic lizard'. The dinosaur was named by Richard Lydekker in 1877 – almost 20 years after its remains were first discovered.

Titanosaurus was a sauropod dionosaur, like Argentinosaurus and Brachiosaurus.

Appearance

Titanosaurus had a bulky body, a long 'whiplash' tail and a tiny head on the end of its long neck. The head was incredibly small compared to the rest of its body, but was quite wide. It had large nostrils, and its nasal bones formed a sort of raised crest on its skull. It had very small teeth.

It grew to around 39–59 ft in length and about 10–16 ft tall at the hips. It would have weighed about 15 tons.

This dinosaur walked on all fours. Its front legs were stout and stocky. Its back legs were longer than the front ones, and Titanosaurus would have been able to rear up onto these strong back legs to reach higher up trees for food. It had a very flexible spine, making rearing up easy.

Dinosaur Data

PRONUNCIATION:	TIE-**TAN**-OH-**SAWR**-US
SUBORDER:	SAUROPODA
FAMILY:	TITANOSAURIDAE
DESCRIPTION:	GIANT ARMORED HERBIVORE
FEATURES:	LONG NECK, FLEXIBLE BACK, ARMOURED SKIN
DIET:	CONIFERS, PALMS, GRASSES

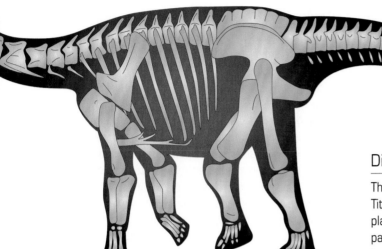

Diet

The fossilized remains of Titanosaur dung show that Titanosaurus had quite a broad diet. It ate pretty much any plant material – remains from conifer twigs and leaves, palms and grasses were all found. Titanosaurus lived in herds, browsing from place to place to find fresh vegetation to eat.

Reproduction

Titanosaurus laid eggs, and the whole herd probably shared one large nesting ground, where they dug nests and then buried their eggs under dirt and vegetation. Their eggs would have measured only 4–5 in. across.

Latest discoveries

In May 2006, Italian scientists announced the discovery of four well-preserved Titanosaur skeletons in South America. There are skeletons of young Titanosaurs as well as adults.

Titanosaurus had a very wide chest, which placed its legs and feet widely apart. Scientists have discovered fossilized footprints (we call these 'fossilized trackways') showing that Titanosaurus tracks are much wider than those of other sauropod dinosaurs.

Fossilized impressions of Titanosaurus' skin have survived, so we know that it had armor to protect it. Its skin was covered with a pattern of small 'bead-like' scales surrounding larger scales.

MEGA FACTS

- Although Titanosaurus eggs were only about 5 in. across, the babies that hatched would grow to be longer than a bus!

- Living in herds would have given Titanosaurus protection against large predators.

NODOSAURUS

Tank-like armored herbivore

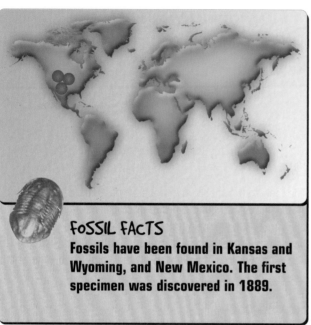

FOSSIL FACTS
Fossils have been found in Kansas and Wyoming, and New Mexico. The first specimen was discovered in 1889.

Appearance

Nodosaurus was 13–20 ft long and grew up to 10 ft high. It moved on four stocky legs, and had five-toed feet. Its front legs were much shorter than its back legs, making its body strongly arched. Its neck was short and its head small.

No Nodosaurus skull has been discovered so its shape has to be deduced from skulls of other nodosaurids. It would probably have had a narrow head, a pointed snout, and powerful jaws with small leaf-shaped teeth back in its cheeks. It may have fed on soft plants. Like other herbivores, it may have swallowed small stones (called gastroliths) to aid with grinding up food in its large gut.

Nodosaurus means 'knobbed lizard' or 'node lizard'. It was named by Othniel Charles Marsh in 1889, and takes its name from the bony armor plates and knobs which covered most of its skin. Bony armor plates like those possessed by nodosaurus are called scutes. It gave its name to the group of ankylosaurs called nodosaurids.

Nodosaurids differ from the other types of ankylosaur in lacking a club at the end of their tail. Nodosaurids were distinguished by the bands of spikes that ran along the sides of their body, pear-shaped heads, and relatively narrow toothless beaks. A bony plate separated their nasal passage from their mouth, so that they could chew food and breathe at the same time.

They had a single large armor plate over the snout, and a solid shield of partially-fused armored plates protecting the pelvic area. For extra protection, they had bony spikes that stuck out from their flanks.

Nodosaurus attacked by lone raptor

Defense

It had armor plating on its back and sides. It had large armored plates topped with bony nodes on the skin between its ribs, and – unlike other nodosaurids – had dorsal armor, consisting of a pair of midline rectangular scutes with domed centres alternating with bands of smaller, flat and square-shaped scutes. It may have had shoulder or side spikes – remains found so far are not enough to tell us for certain.

Nodosaurus had little means of attacking an enemy. If attacked, it probably relied on crouching low to the ground to protect its soft underside.

MEGA FACTS

- Nodosorous had a small head and minuscule brain compared to the size of its body, indicating very low intelligence.

- In 2003, the fossilized skeleton of an armoured dinosaur that may be a Nodosaurus was found in Kent, England. Except for the missing skull, it is remarkably complete. Only further study will tell us for certain if this is the first Nodosaurus found outside America.

Dinosaur Data

PRONUNCIATION:	NOH-DOH-**SAWR**-US
SUBORDER:	THYREOPHORA
FAMILY:	NODOSAURIDAE
DESCRIPTION:	ARMORED HERBIVORE

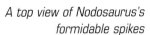

A top view of Nodosaurus's formidable spikes

MINMI

Small and unusual armored herbivore

This dinosaur was named and described by Ralph Molnar in 1980. It was named after the place where the first pieces of its fossil remains had been found, Minmi Crossing.

Minmi was the first armored dinosaur found south of the equator. It is also the most complete dinosaur skeleton ever found in Australia.

Appearance

Minmi seems to have been a very primitive ankylosaur and scientists have found it hard to classify. It has features in common with both ankylosaurs and nodosaurs, but is not identical to either. Its snout arched higher than the rest of its skull, which is common in nodosaurs. It had armoured plates like an ankylosaur's – but its legs were longer, and it had no 'club' at the end of its tail.

It would have been about the size of a year-old calf, growing to only 6–10 ft long and about 3 ft high, and weighing around 3,740 lb. Its back legs were longer than its front ones, and it went on all fours. Minmi would have lived on the low-growing plants of the floodplains and woodlands where it roamed.

As well as having longer legs than ankylosaurus, Minmi had extra bony plates added to its backbone. These strengthened its back, helping support the weight of its armour. Extra muscles attached to these extra plates could have allowed Minmi to run at reasonable speed.

Defense

Minmi had skin armored with large bony plates (called scutes) and smaller pea-sized bones (called ossicles) embedded all over it. Even Minmi's underbelly was protected by small bony plates, which makes it unique among the whole thyreophoran suborder of dinosaurs.

Apart from this armor, Minmi had no real way to defend itself – it lacked the tail 'club' possessed by most ankylosaurs. Running away was probably its best defence!

Minmi was the only ankylosaur to have paravertebrae. Some scientists have suggested that these are actually tendons which have ossified (changed into bone) rather than true bones.

FOSSIL FACTS
Fossils have been found in Queensland, Australia. The first fossils were discovered by Alan Batholomai near Roma, Queensland in 1964.

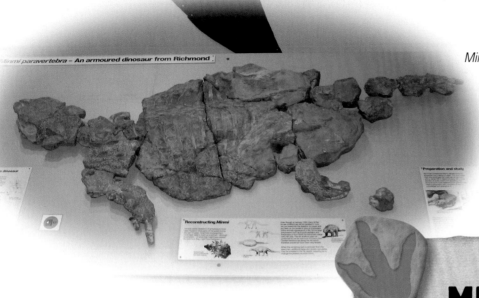

Minmi skeleton

Minmi has much in common with both ankylosaurs and nodosaurs, but it may turn out to be a wholly new type of armored dinosaur!

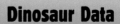

MEGA FACTS

- In 1990 an almost-complete Minmi skeleton was found in Queensland. It was so well preserved that wrinkles in its skin could be made out from the pattern of the ossicles.

- Minmi has the shortest name ever given to a dinosaur.

- Recent studies have been able to analyse the contents of a Minmi stomach. It was able to chew its food into smaller pieces before swallowing them.

Dinosaur Data

PRONUNCIATION:	**MIN**-MEE
SUBORDER:	THYREOPHORA
DESCRIPTION:	SMALL ARMORED HERBIVORE
FEATURES:	ARMORED PLATES ON BELLY
DIET:	LOW-GROWING SOFT PANTS MATERIALS, LEAVES, FRUIT, STEMS

CAMARASAURUS

Giant herbivore

FOSSIL FACTS
Camarasaurus fossils have been
found in North America.
Ultrasaurus fossils have been found
in the USA and Asia.

Dinosaur Data

PRONUNCIATION:	KUH-**MARE**-UH-**SAWR**-US
SUBORDER:	SAUROPODOMORPHA
FAMILY:	CAMARASAURIDAE
DESCRIPTION:	A GIANT HERBIVORE
FEATURES:	SPOON-SHAPED TEETH
DIET:	PLANTS

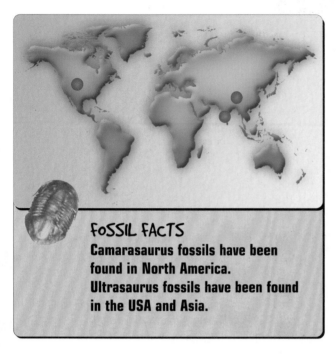

Camarasaurus lived during the
late Jurassic Period, about
155 to 145 million
years ago.

Camarasaurus looked very much like
Diplodocus with its long neck and tail. It was
a giant herbivore, but it wasn't as big as
other sauropods. It still weighed up to
20 tons!

Its head was small and long, and it had a blunt snout. It had
spoon-shaped teeth, which were ideal for munching on
leaves and branches.

Camarasaurus fossils have been found in groups with both
adult and young together. They probably traveled together in
herds like elephants.

JUL 0 7 2014

Date Due

BRODART, CO.   Cat. No. 23-233   Printed in U.S.A.

A volume in the series *The Culture and Politics of Health Care Work*

Edited by **Suzanne Gordon** and **Sioban Nelson**

For a list of books in the series, visit our website at **www.cornellpress.cornell.edu**

Creating the Health Care Team of the Future

The Toronto Model for Interprofessional Education and Practice

Sioban Nelson, Maria Tassone,

and Brian D. Hodges

ILR Press

an imprint of

Cornell University Press

Ithaca and London

First published 2014 by Cornell University Press
First printing, Cornell Paperbacks, 2014

Printed in the United States of America

Library of Congress Cataloging-in-Publication Data

Nelson, Sioban, author.
    Creating the health care team of the future: the Toronto Model for interprofessional education and practice / Sioban Nelson, Maria Tassone, and Brian D. Hodges.
        pages cm. -- (The culture and politics of health care work)
        Includes bibliographical references and index.
        ISBN 978-0-8014-5300-7 (cloth : alk. paper) --
        ISBN 978-0-8014-7941-0 (pbk. : alk. paper)

1. Medicine--Study and teaching (Continuing education)--Ontario--Toronto. 2. Health care teams--Training of--Ontario--Toronto. 3. Interprofessional relations--Study and teaching (Continuing education)--Ontario--Toronto. I. Tassone, Maria, 1968- author. II. Hodges, Brian David, 1964- author. III. Title.

        R845.N45 2014
        610.9713'541--dc23   2013043153

Cornell University Press strives to use environmentally responsible suppliers and materials to the fullest extent possible in the publishing of its books. Such materials include vegetable-based, low-VOC inks and acid-free papers that are recycled, totally chlorine-free, or partly composed of nonwood fibers. For further information, visit our website at www.cornellpress.cornell.edu.

Cloth printing   10 9 8 7 6 5 4 3 2 1
Paperback printing   10 9 8 7 6 5 4 3 2 1

Contents

Acknowledgements

THE AUTHORS FOR THE WORKBOOK PERSONIFY THE UNIVERSITY–
clinical partnership that is at the heart of the Toronto
Model, the University of Toronto's approach to interprofessional education and care (IPE/C); Sioban Nelson, Vice
Provost Academic Programs, University of Toronto; Maria
Tassone, Director of the Centre for Interprofessional Education and Assistant Professor, Department of Physical Therapy,
Faculty of Medicine at the University of Toronto; and Senior
Director, Interprofessional Education & Care at the University Health Network; and Brian Hodges, Vice President Education at the University Health Network, professor, Department of Psychiatry at the University of Toronto, Scientist at
the Wilson Centre for Research in Education. Each of the affiliated teaching hospitals and health professional faculties of
the university–hospital partnership participated in the project
by furnishing case studies of their IPE/C activities and linking
the workbook team with educators, clinicians, students, and
patients who could provide their perspectives and enrich the
text with examples of creativity and innovation. The full list
of those who were part of this collaborative project and the
nature of their contribution is provided below.

The project was made possible through the support of the
Deans of the Health Sciences at the University of Toronto (U of
T) and the CEOs of the Toronto Academic Health Science Network (TAHSN). Their collective support, both financial and
moral, was critical to garner the participation and enthusiasm
of faculty, clinicians, patients, and students in the project.

Many of those who began the work that evolved into the
Toronto Model from the 1990s have subsequently moved on,
but the work has been carried forward by new generations of
IPE/C focused teachers and practitioners. In this book we have
tried to honour the many hands and multiple ideas that creat-

ed both the opportunity for IPE/C at U of T and the eventual program. Writers Susan Pedwell and Dave Ross were engaged in interviewing stakeholders to get the background and context straight. Another writer, Sydney Goodfellow, interviewed student groups and visited the student-run Interprofessional Medical and Allied Groups for Improving Neighbourhood Environments Clinic, better known as the IMAGINE Clinic. The patient perspective was provided by individuals affiliated with the Health Mentor Program and the *ehpic*™ program at the U of T, and the Patient Educator Program at Holland Bloorview Kids Rehabilitation Hospital. Interview materials have been integrated as narrative in each of the chapters, as well as in pull-out quotes that reflect the diversity of stakeholders and voices. Although the narrative has been woven together from individual interviews, the IPE/C program and its growth and success have been the result of thousands of people in Toronto, a true team effort.

We are deeply indebted to former and current Centre for IPE faculty and staff for all the assistance they have provided, and in particular for the valuable insights and thoughtful edits as the book evolved. We would like to thank Ivy Oandasan, the key leader in interprofessional education when we began on this road. Ivy has generously provided detailed feedback on the manuscript and offered suggestions that have enhanced it greatly. Dave Ross was the project officer, and he did a fantastic job holding the thousands of pieces together. Sofia Martimianakis and Alexandra Harris compiled the annotated bibliography, as well as assisted in pulling together the final manuscript. Gil Martinez was enormously helpful in assisting us to organize the material visually, adapting and developing figures, and transforming the text to a workbook. Liz Ross provided a careful edit of the manuscript prior to submission. Suzanne Gordon has been a champion of this project from the start. The book was entirely her idea. She read the draft manuscript thoroughly and provided helpful, detailed feedback.

Our greatest thanks go to all the hundred or so individuals who generously provided written material, personal recollections, and information for this project. So many people have worked tirelessly to develop a new way of practice and to support the next generation of health professionals to function as collaborative team members who can work effectively to meet the needs of patients and families. It has been a great privilege for the editors to tell their collective story.

Case studies were provided by partners from across the Toronto Academic Health Science Network. Ruth Barker of Sunnybrook Health Sciences Centre contributed "A Story of Energy

and Enthusiasm—Interprofessional Education at Sunnybrook Health Sciences Centre." Faith Boutcher of Baycrest provided "The Centre for Learning, Research and Innovation." Dale Kuehl from the Centre for Addiction and Mental Health provided "Transforming the Lives of People with Mental Health Problems." Paula Rowland of Toronto East General Hospital contributed information on partnership councils. Andrea Cameron wrote "Teamwork—Your Future in Interprofessional Health Care" in the Faculty of Pharmacy. A study on the "Dying and Death Seminar" from the Faculty of Social Work was provided by Michele Chaban. Bonnie Fleming-Carroll of the Hospital for Sick Children profiled the "Partnered Learning Project: A Study in Interprofessional Collaboration and Learning." Patricia Houston and Rob Fox from St. Michael's Hospital wrote on the Student Experience Committee and its role in IPE education at the Li Ka Shing International Healthcare Education Centre. Karen Gold from Women's College Hospital contributed information on the Intimate Partner Abuse learning activity, and worked with Mandy Lowe of the Centre for IPE and Patti McGillicuddy from the University Health Network to contribute "Handle with Care: Do You Know How? – Using Reader's Theatre to Surface Interprofessional Ethics, Values, and Care Relationships." Darlene Hubley from Holland Bloorview Kids Rehabilitation Hospital provided "Exploring Patients and Families in IPE Teaching and Learning." St. Joseph's Health Centre and Elizabeth McLaney profiled their Interprofessional Skills Fair. Rick Penciner and Susan Woollard of North York General Hospital outlined their iPed faculty development programming. Donna Romano from Mount Sinai Hospital profiled Interprofessional Team Check-Ins on Inpatient Psychiatry. Jay Rosenfield from the Faculty of Medicine addressed IPE in the Transition to Clerkship and Residency learning activities. Dr. Gajanan Kulkarni from the Faculty of Dentistry provided "Infant and Child Oral Health Promotion: A New Dentistry-Led Interprofessional Education Initiative." Finally, Tracy Paulenko contributed information on the creation of IPE Structured Placements at Toronto Rehab, now part of the University Health Network.

Interviews were conducted with the following individuals: from Baycrest, Jennifer Reguindin and Karima Velji; from the Centre for Addiction and Mental Health, Susan Morris, Ivan Silver, and Rani Srivastava; from the Centre for IPE, Maria Tassone, Mandy Lowe, Sylvia Langlois, Dante Morra, Ivy Oandasan, Lynne Sinclair, and Susan Wagner; from the Faculty of Dentistry, Daniel Haas; from Holland Bloorview Kids Rehabilitation Hospital, Golda Milo-Manson, Kathryn Parker, Darlene Hubley, and Crystal Chin; from the student-run

IMAGINE clinic, Yick Kan Cheung, Enoch Ng, Michael Bonores, and Mahwesh Saddiqi; from the Interprofessional Healthcare Students' Association IPHSA, Nikki Fischer, Kaspar Ng, and Elisa Simpson; from KPMG Global Centre of Excellence for Health, Mark Rochon; from the Faculty of Medicine at the University of Toronto, Catharine Whiteside, Sarita Verma, Salvatore Spadafora, and Jay Rosenfield; from Mount Sinai Hospital, Donna Romano and Virginia Fernandes; from the Faculty of Nursing at the University of Toronto, Maureen Barry, Sioban Nelson, Freida Chavez, and Judy Watt-Watson; from the Faculty of Pharmacy, Henry Mann, Andrea Cameron, and Wayne Hindmarsh; from the Faculty of Social Work, Faye Mishna and Michele Chaban; from Sunnybrook Health Sciences Centre, Joshua Tepper; from the University Health Network, Brian Hodges, Mandy Lowe, Patti McGillicuddy, and Emily Lap Sum Musing; from St. Michael's Hospital, Patricia Houston and Rob Fox; from the Hospital for Sick Children, Bonnie Fleming-Carroll; from St. Joseph's Health Centre, Elizabeth McLaney; and from Women's College Hospital, Karen Gold. We are also grateful for the interviews held with our Patient Mentors, who have chosen to remain anonymous.

Creating the
Health Care Team
of the Future

Why a Toronto Model Workbook?

I
N THE SPRING OF 2012, WHEN A GROUP OF UNIVERSITY OF TORON-
to Centre for Interprofessional Education faculty finished
up a workshop at Indiana University, they got a big surprise:
the forty participants simultaneously rose to their feet and
applauded. The senior academic leaders in medicine and nursing present at the workshop were clapping excitedly about the
interprofessional education (IPE) training program they had
just completed.

What evoked a standing ovation from an audience that day
in Indiana? A small group of dedicated IPE proponents had
successfully convinced the University of Toronto's health faculties and teaching hospitals that to best serve the needs of
complex patients, better promote health, improve quality, and
increase patient safety, they needed to adopt a new model of
education and practice—interprofessional education and care
(IPE/C). The audience response was also inspired by the willingness of the Toronto team to share not only their successes
but their frustrations, mistakes, wrong turns, and solutions
to the vexing problems that many of those struggling to establish IPE programs share. This response also reflected the
audience's desire to respond to the problems of patient safety,
job stress and caregiver burnout, and escalating health care
costs that have been highlighted in countless reports over the
past two decades.

In 2000, the Institute of Medicine's landmark report *To Err
Is Human*[1] launched the contemporary patient safety movement with its clarion call to the health care systems all over
the globe to act to prevent the errors that kill over 100,000
patients a year and harm many thousands more in the United
States alone. Ten years later, in 2010, the World Health Organization's (WHO) "Framework for Action on Interprofes-

sional Education and Collaborative Practice"[2] was released, as was the Lancet Commission report "Health Professionals for a New Century: Transforming Education to Strengthen Health Systems in an Interdependent World."[3] In fact, over the past decade or more, studies have documented that, far from improving, in countries such as the United States and Canada, there has been little progress in preventing patient deaths and harm. Original calculations such as those done by the Institute of Medicine in 2000 are now considered to have been dramatic underestimations of the harm done to patients in health care institutions around the world.

Although the complexity of today's high-tech health care systems is often used as a rationalization for the maintenance of the status quo, all these groundbreaking reports argue that team-based, or *interprofessional*, care is a key strategy to move our current underperforming health care systems toward a more safe, efficient, integrated, and cost-effective model. Contemporary health care institutions do indeed have a bewildering number of players. Despite this, the responsibility for ensuring that patients receive the right care at the right time from the right providers relies on a few basic principles:

1. Practitioners need to understand they are part of a diverse team.
2. Practitioners must communicate effectively with the patient and family, as well as with other members of their team.
3. Practitioners need to know what other team members do to limit duplication and prevent gaps in care.
4. Practitioners need to know how to work together to optimize care so that the patient journey from inpatient care to home care, or from primary care to the specialist clinic is experienced as seamless.

None of this can happen if there is no education in teamwork from the very beginning of the health care professional's educational journey—in a health professional school—and if that education is not continued throughout their entire career in whatever practice setting they work in. Since the traditional education of the health care professional has most often taken place in siloed programs that have little connection to one another, and traditional care tends to involve parallel play in the practice setting, it has become clear to those concerned with patient safety and health care education that a profound culture change is required to produce interprofessional care and optimal teamwork.[4] Patient safety will improve only when we change the way health professionals relate to each other, the

way they see themselves in relation to members of their own profession and to colleagues from other disciplines. This kind of change cannot be an abstract classroom exercise. It must be learned, modeled, and reinforced. There must be organizational commitment and professional willingness to go down this path of partnership between education and practice. But first there must be an education program that starts learners on this road and brings them together with mentors who are committed to new ways of delivering care and working together.

All over the world, educators and practitioners are beginning to recognize this and have embarked on efforts to set up interprofessional education and practice programs. In response to these influential calls for a new way of practice and new models of education, health professional programs across North America have begun to pilot programs that introduced collaborative learning opportunities into their curricula. The Josiah Macy Jr. Foundation has been a major supporter of this movement, seeding educational initiatives across the United States through their funding program and supporting faculty development through their fellowship program. Accreditation and certification agencies have likewise supported this shift. In 2012, the Liaison Committee on Medical Education (LCME) adopted a new accreditation standard (ED-19-A) that will come into effect in 2015 for medical schools in North America.[5] This standard will require all medical education programs in the United States to prepare students to function collaboratively on health care teams that include other health professionals. For their part, hospitals and other health care settings are being similarly challenged to fulfill their mandate to begin to practice in a more interprofessional way and to conduct in-house education to teach clinicians and other health care workers how to do so.

This transition of IPE from "nice to do" to "must do" has, not surprisingly, been accompanied by an enormous upsurge in interest in models of IPE/C from the many health professional schools struggling to respond to the new mandate to include interprofessional education in their curricula, often with little guidance or support. That is why we have written this workbook.

Since 2000, the eleven health professional programs at the University of Toronto and the forty-nine teaching hospitals associated with them have developed an Interprofessional Education and Care (IPE/C) program that begins in the first year of a health professional student's entry into his or her program, continues through various educational activities throughout their studies, and straddles the education/prac-

tice divide. Over the past decade, the university and teaching hospital partners have been engaged in the co-development and support of the IPE curriculum for learners. They are also investing in the development of faculty and the ongoing training of staff to support and model collaborative practice and team-based care. What we have come to think of as the "Toronto Model" is integrated across all sites and professions and includes classroom, simulation, and practice education.

The Toronto Model has been developed through trial and error over the past decade. But how did we move from a series of abstract principles to an impressive array of concrete programs that span educational and practice institutions? This is the question Maria Tassone, the director of the Centre for Interprofessional Education, is always asked when she speaks about the activities at Toronto in North America and around the world (see Figure 2). This and other frequently asked questions (FAQs) that educators and practitioners all over the world ask Tassone and others at the university are what inspired this book and form its core. Everyone, it seems, wants to know:

- How did you start?
- How did you get everyone to participate?
- How did you find common curriculum time?
- How did you make it mandatory?
- How did you find placements? How did you find faculty?
- How do you continue to grow and sustain this work in education and practice?

We decided to focus this book on these practical questions. This is not to say our approach has been atheoretical or unscientific. However, we have found that presenting a lot of theory does not help people struggling to figure out what to teach, how to teach it, and how to begin to travel down the challenging and meaningful road of changing both pedagogy and practice.

What we have tried to do in this workbook is capture the collective activity and creativity, and to relay the outcomes and lessons learned. We do not wish to suggest that these successes are the result of individual initiatives or that others simply replicate what we have done; rather, we aim to share lessons learned and show how this collective work has been fundamental to the successes achieved thus far. Every school or service provider will have its own cultural specifications to which an IPE/C approach must be adapted. We can share what our issues were and how we managed them.

This workbook is geared toward a broad audience of health professional teachers (pre- and post licensure) charged with

revising curricula to include interprofessional components, as well as to clinical faculty who are introducing IPE/C in their clinical training programs and professional development activities. It also addresses those who are charged with enhancing quality and patient safety—and even patient satisfaction—in their institutions. It is drawn from the experiences of faculty, clinical teachers, and health care practitioners across university and practice settings and across all the health sciences.

What worked for us, as well as what did not, is at the core of this text. As professional programs and service providers struggle to both create and train teams of health professionals that are willing and able to work together, and to raise the bar with respect to service integration and better patient care, we share how far we have come along this path. These lessons may be helpful for those who are just setting out and wondering where to start. Or, if you have been building bridges and getting things moving, but are not sure how to take the program forward to build interprofessional approaches to care, this book aims to help. "Scaling up" is a common challenge in IPE/C; that is, how to move from innovative pilot studies to systemwide change. At the University of Toronto we have moved beyond the "thousand points of light" of innovations to a formally mandated curriculum that has made IPE a core component of what it means to be a health sciences student. The journey is not over; the end is not even close. But along the way we are learning about the power of process, collaboration, and collective vision. For the thousands of educators and clinicians all over the world on a similar journey, we share our efforts.

Through the case studies we present different kinds of curricula, teams, and clinical settings. We provide insights on how to get started and the important role of champions in cultural change. Some of these case studies are presented in the narrative, while others are pull-out case studies, side columns, and boxes. These design features are to facilitate the "drop in, drop out" nature of the text. For those interested in the theoretical and methodological aspects of IPE/C program development, we have added a Further Reading section at the end of the book, which provides detail on selected published work that has been produced over the years by Toronto faculty. We would also direct readers to the key journal in the field of IPE/C, the *Journal of Interprofessional Care*.

Over the years, the Centre for IPE has built an impressive array of tools to assist the process of implementing IPE/C into diverse environments and to build capacity through educate-the-educator approaches. In this workbook we provide some of these basic tools and information. We also provide

QR Codes (matrix, or two-dimensional, barcode) in the margins for the reader to link directly with more extensive and continually updated resources on the website.

These resources are much requested, heavily accessed from our website, and disseminated through multiple workshops and education programs offered around the world. But people want more. The Centre for IPE is being constantly contacted directly by those downloading the resource material who love the resources but are not sure how to apply them to their specific context, or even where to begin. This workbook responds to this need by guiding the reader step-by-step through the various aspects of program development and implementation. The workbook provides an integrated framework through which to decide what tools are appropriate for your program and a guide for how to use them.

A workbook is not intended to be read sequentially or at one sitting. The emphasis is on "how to," and areas of interest will vary both among readers and, over time, for individual readers. Thus some of the descriptive material is intentionally repetitive to demonstrate core principles and process issues that must be dealt with in varying sites and contexts, with different clinical populations and different constellations of team members. The goal is to facilitate the reader's ability to work with the examples that are most relevant to their needs.

Finally, a note on evaluation of IPE/C and outcome data. Interprofessional education is an emerging field, and we are at the beginning stages of a mass movement. The University of Toronto is a global leader in IPE/C and yet, even for us, the full mandatory curriculum is barely four years old. While we are constantly evaluating these programs, it is not yet possible for us to state what outcomes they have produced at this stage of development. That said, the current priority for Toronto and other IPE programs around the world is to develop an evaluative framework and build the data sets. It will come. Right now we are on the cusp of having the critical mass necessary to generate robust data, and we expect to see very different discussion around IPE/C over the next decade. What we can say is that all around the world people are struggling with the problem of how to bring large-scale paradigm-breaking change without the "evidence" usually required to justify such change. We believe the program at Toronto is, in itself, a major outcome. It has been implemented, is supported, and has become a core mission for both the university and the clinical setting—no small feat. This book provides an analysis of what led to that outcome.

In the spirit of IPE/C, multiple voices are heard in this book. Contributors range from undergraduate students to senior

clinicians. Stakeholders include service providers, administrators, deans, CEOs, faculty, patients, and point-of-care clinicians. While that may appear an unwieldy and eclectic mix, it mirrors the complexity and diversity of the health care system. Figuring out how to help all these players align into high-functioning teams, configured to optimally meet patient and client needs, is the daily challenge of health care around the world.

Many of the IPE activities described in this workbook directly engage patients and clients as facilitators, curriculum developers, and consultants. Capturing that patient/client voice has been an important commitment in this book. Similarly, students have been an integral part of the story in Toronto, and their voices are also reflected in the IPE/C journey.

A NOTE ON TERMINOLOGY

Team-based care, *collaborative practice*, and *interprofessional care* are terms that are often used interchangeably in the literature. The University of Toronto has adopted the WHO operational definition for *interprofessional education*: "Interprofessional education occurs when two or more professions learn about, from and with each other to enable effective collaboration and improve health outcomes."[6]

Furthermore, we characterize *interprofessional collaboration* as the integration and modification of different professions' contributions in light of input from other professions. Rather than merely learning *with* other health professional students, the hallmark of IPE is the cognitive and behavioral change that occurs in participants who develop an understanding of the core principles and concepts of each contributing discipline and are familiar with the basic language and mindsets of the various disciplines.

In terms of *interprofessional care*, we use the Ontario Ministry of Health and Long Term Care definition of the provision of comprehensive health services to patients by multiple health caregivers who work collaboratively to deliver quality care within and across settings.[7]

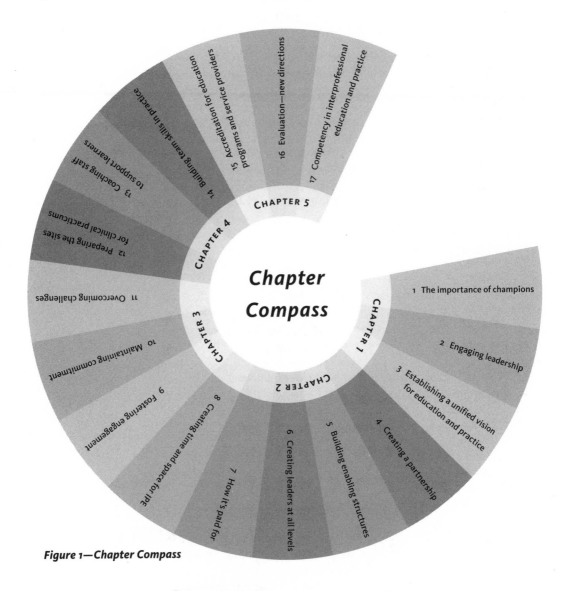

Figure 1—Chapter Compass

ORGANIZATION

The book is organized into five chapters. A compass illustration guides the reader at the beginning of each chapter (see Figure 1).

Chapter 1 provides the history and the impetus that propelled educators and clinicians at the University of Toronto to begin this journey. It demonstrates that a broad group of committed leaders was integral to the launch of such an ambitious plan. Catharine Whiteside, the current dean of the Faculty of Medicine and vice-provost, Relations with Health Care Institutions, was a standout leader in this initiative; as a result, medicine has been front and center to the IPE/C program at

Toronto. The deans from the Council of Health Science Deans (as it was then called), led by Wayne Hindmarsh, the dean of Pharmacy at the time, were fully in support of the IPE/C initiative, as were the CEOs of the teaching hospitals. These leaders recruited Ivy Oandasan to the role of director of the Office of Interprofessional Education at the University of Toronto, with the task of making IPE a reality across the hospitals and across the health professional programs. Without that strong commitment from the leadership at both the University and the practice settings, it is difficult to see how IPE/C could ever have moved from the periphery to the mainstream of health professional education at Toronto.

Chapter 2 describes the structure of the University of Toronto. It outlines the programs, partners, and relationships between the teaching hospitals and the various university programs, as well as within the university overall. It gives the contextual information necessary to understand the overlapping field between the university and the teaching hospitals that compose the Toronto Academic Health Science Network (TAHSN), and this network constitutes the greatest distinguishing feature of Toronto and its model of IPE/C.

However, culture change is not a top-down exercise. Senior leadership is required to sanction the efforts and, where necessary, to resource them. For a program that involves all health professional programs at all clinical sites to be instituted, there has to be an army of willing innovators and pioneers leading from where they stand, in both formal and informal leadership roles. Creating and sustaining the energy and enthusiasm of these champions involves structures and processes for building a cross-cutting curriculum and creating a new type of practice. Once that is accomplished, the hurdle becomes that of implementing the content and IPE/C opportunities into overcrowded and pressured curricula.

Of all the questions educators from around the world ask of Toronto, the key question is: "How did you create space in the curriculum for this?" **Chapter 3** deals squarely with this question, addressing the political economy of curriculum time, negotiating space, and maintaining the engagement of champions and faculty to ensure the commitment continues even as faces change around the table. We present what the actual IPE curriculum looks like and how it was created, approved, and implemented. One of the important strategies in negotiating precious curriculum space and time was the development of core and elective curriculum components. These elective components are enormously varied and offer something for everyone. We have electives developed and conducted on campus, while others are offered in the teach-

ing hospitals; one of the examples we share was developed and is run by students.

Chapter 4 examines the implementation of IPE/C beyond the university and focuses on the clinical setting. We know how quickly lessons learned in the "ivory tower" can be scuttled by the "hidden curriculum" enacted daily in the workplace. How does one prepare clinical preceptors and faculty for a cohort of students being educated in a new way? How do the multiple clinical programs, professional training programs, and services begin to engage in IPE/C? What kind of experiences can be developed for prelicensure learners, postgraduate and graduate trainees, and staff professional development programs? In this chapter the diversity of TAHSN allows for a rich variety of examples of innovation. From the large comprehensive hospitals such as the University Health Network and St. Michael's Hospital, to the specialist service providers such as the Centre for Addiction and Mental Health, the Hospital for Sick Children, and Holland Bloorview Kids Rehabili-

Reach of Toronto Model

Figure 2—Represents select workshops, seminars, consultations and research collaborations with the Centre for Interprofessional Education

tation Hospital, to community hospitals such as North York General and Toronto East General Hospital, the hospitals all offer IPE initiatives to student learners, and coach staff to better support these learners, and to build the team effectiveness of their staff to improve care.

Chapter 5 looks at the most recent thinking in IPE/C and discusses the implications for accreditation for programs and hospitals, competency frameworks within and across professions, and directions in evaluation for learning and patient/client outcomes. The idea that is gaining currency across the world, as demonstrated in Figure 2, is that we need teams of interprofessional providers to address health promotion and wellness, the social determinants of health, chronic disease self-management and management, and acute episodic care. For team care to become institutionalized as the "new normal," the mechanisms that oversee training, accreditation, and regulation of health professional programs need to fully engage. Already there is evidence that this is happening, and much of the recent debate

on health professional education reform is premised on the notion that teams are the preferred future.

In what follows we offer the story, the tools and our lessons learned in the spirit of collaboration and sharing. We look forward to supporting those who are just beginning this journey, as well as those who may be "stuck" at the stage of multiple small initiatives with no systemwide traction. Others who have well-developed and sophisticated IPE/C programs in place may find this book a source of different ideas or approaches they may wish to try. Interprofessional education and care is about living the message of collaboration and the belief that no one has anything to lose from sharing. This workbook has been produced in that spirit.

CHAPTER 1

Getting Started

FIRST—LOOK AT YOUR CONTEXT

UNDERSTANDING YOUR CONTEXT IS KEY STARTING DOWN THE PATH of IPE. In order to share the Toronto Model, we must first describe our context and our structures, and the types of programs, learners, and clinical partners that characterize health professional education at Toronto. More broadly the rise of IPE in Canada was stimulated by a series of key federal and provincial (or state) initiatives that provided the impetus for early adopters. In this chapter we share how we began.

WHAT DOES THE TORONTO LANDSCAPE LOOK LIKE?

The University of Toronto (U of T) is a large public research–intensive university with 80,000 plus students and 11,500 faculty. We have a large medical program with nearly 1,000 undergraduate students, 3,000 graduate students, 2,000 residents, and 3,000 postdoctoral and MD clinical fellows[1] and partner with dozens of affiliated hospitals (teaching and community hospitals). In Ontario alone, one third of all family doctors have received training at U of T, and nationwide, one quarter of all medical specialists did all or some of their training here.[2] Medical education therefore features prominently in the U of T story. The Faculty of Medicine also includes five distinct health science programs: medical radiation science, occupational science and occupational therapy, physical therapy, physician assistant, and speech-language pathology. The faculties of dentistry, kinesiology and physical education, nursing, pharmacy, and social work are by comparison much smaller than medicine. Nursing, for instance, is about a tenth the size of medicine overall at Toronto (see Figure 3).

HIGHLIGHTS

1 The importance of champions

2 Engaging leadership

3 Establishing a unified vision for education and practice

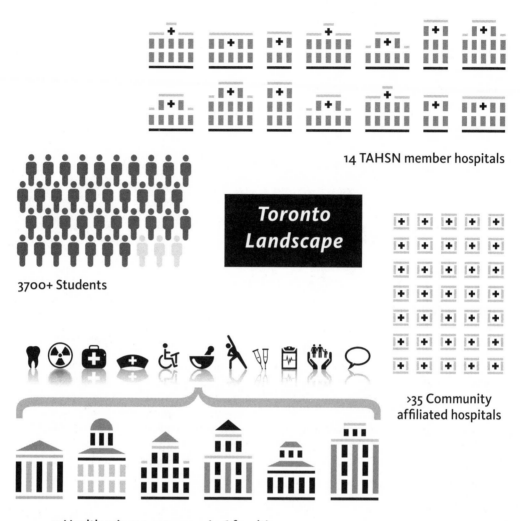

14 TAHSN member hospitals

3700+ Students

Toronto Landscape

›35 Community affiliated hospitals

11 Health science programs in 6 faculties

Figure 3—The elements of IPE at Toronto

http://www.tahsn.ca

In addition to size, the nature of the academic health science centre at U of T is unique. The Toronto Academic Health Science Network (TAHSN) is characterized by a strongly integrated set of linkages that functionally connect leaders in the hospitals with their academic partners at the university. The university doesn't own or run the hospitals, as happens in some academic health science centres around the world. The U of T and the teaching hospitals form a consortium that is based on health professional education and research. This mix of strong sovereign identities among many partners, along with a cohesive purpose around education and research, is what

makes TAHSN complex to maneuver and rich in potential. Every physician is appointed to the university, as are many hundreds of other health professionals. These appointments may be paid; many are unpaid. Appointments may come with teaching expectations or clinical supervision and mentorship, whereas others are largely research-focused.

What Are Our Students Like?

Ten of the eleven health science programs at U of T (with the exception of kinesiology and physical education) are second-entry undergraduate or graduate programs, so students have undertaken university studies prior to entering their health science program. Typically the students have completed an undergraduate degree and, for some, a master's degree (nursing, medicine, pharmacy, and dentistry fit this model). Other programs (such as rehabilitation sciences and social work) are offered only at the graduate level. What this means is that students tend to be roughly the same age—mid- to late twenties on average. The relative maturity of U of T students, we believe, becomes significant when students share learning and team activities.

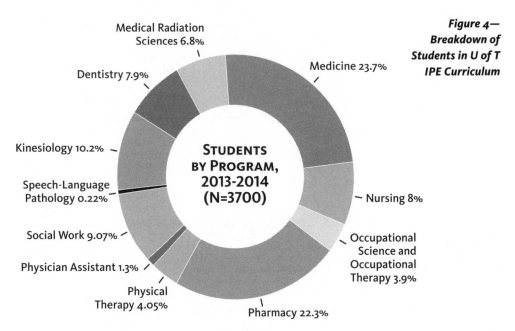

Figure 4—Breakdown of Students in U of T IPE Curriculum

Medical Radiation Sciences 6.8%
Dentistry 7.9%
Kinesiology 10.2%
Speech-Language Pathology 0.22%
Social Work 9.07%
Physician Assistant 1.3%
Physical Therapy 4.05%
Pharmacy 22.3%
Occupational Science and Occupational Therapy 3.9%
Nursing 8%
Medicine 23.7%

Students by Program, 2013-2014 (N=3700)

The IPE Program

The scale of interprofessional education and care (IPE/C) in Toronto is remarkable. There are approximately 3,700 learners engaging in over 120 IPE learning activities offered across

"It's an absolute necessity for the accreditation standards to embrace interprofessionalism and IPE. The curriculum is absolutely packed. Accreditation standards drive curriculum planning, delivery and evaluation. If we're serious about linking our curriculum to the vision of truly improving health, we have to create standards around interprofessionalism that are specifically articulated, delivered and evaluated."

– Catherine Whiteside,
 the dean of Medicine at U of T

eleven professional programs in partnership with fourteen fully affiliated teaching hospitals and approximately thirty-five community hospital affiliated sites. Each year, these learning activities are supported by 620 mentors made up of student facilitators (30), IPE facilitators for practice-sector learning activities (150), and IPE facilitators for university-based learning activities (440) (see Figure 4).

At Toronto, IPE/C is not marginal—it is mainstream. There are teaching, practice, and leadership awards for faculty and students; a student association and a student-run clinic; faculty positions; teacher and clinician education; and leadership development programs. Students learn about, with, and from each other, and they learn how to work together in teams. They then get to practice in both academic and clinical settings.

For the most part, the IPE curriculum is an enhancement of the uni-professional learning (i.e., learning within a single profession) that students undertake in each of their accredited programs. We are fully aware that it is not enough to simply put learners from different disciplines in the same class. We start from the philosophy that team learning needs to be an active component of the curriculum in order for the learning to be directed to improved team outcomes.

SETTING THE STAGE FOR IPE IN TORONTO

EARLY EFFORTS

Health professional students learning together and practicing in teams is not a new idea. Over the course of the twentieth century, various experimental and model programs introduced co-learning and combined learning in which students from different health professional programs may sit in lecture theatres together learning anatomy or ethics. Students often learn in multidisciplinary groups to solve problem-based learning exercises, or they may be placed in teams, such as mental

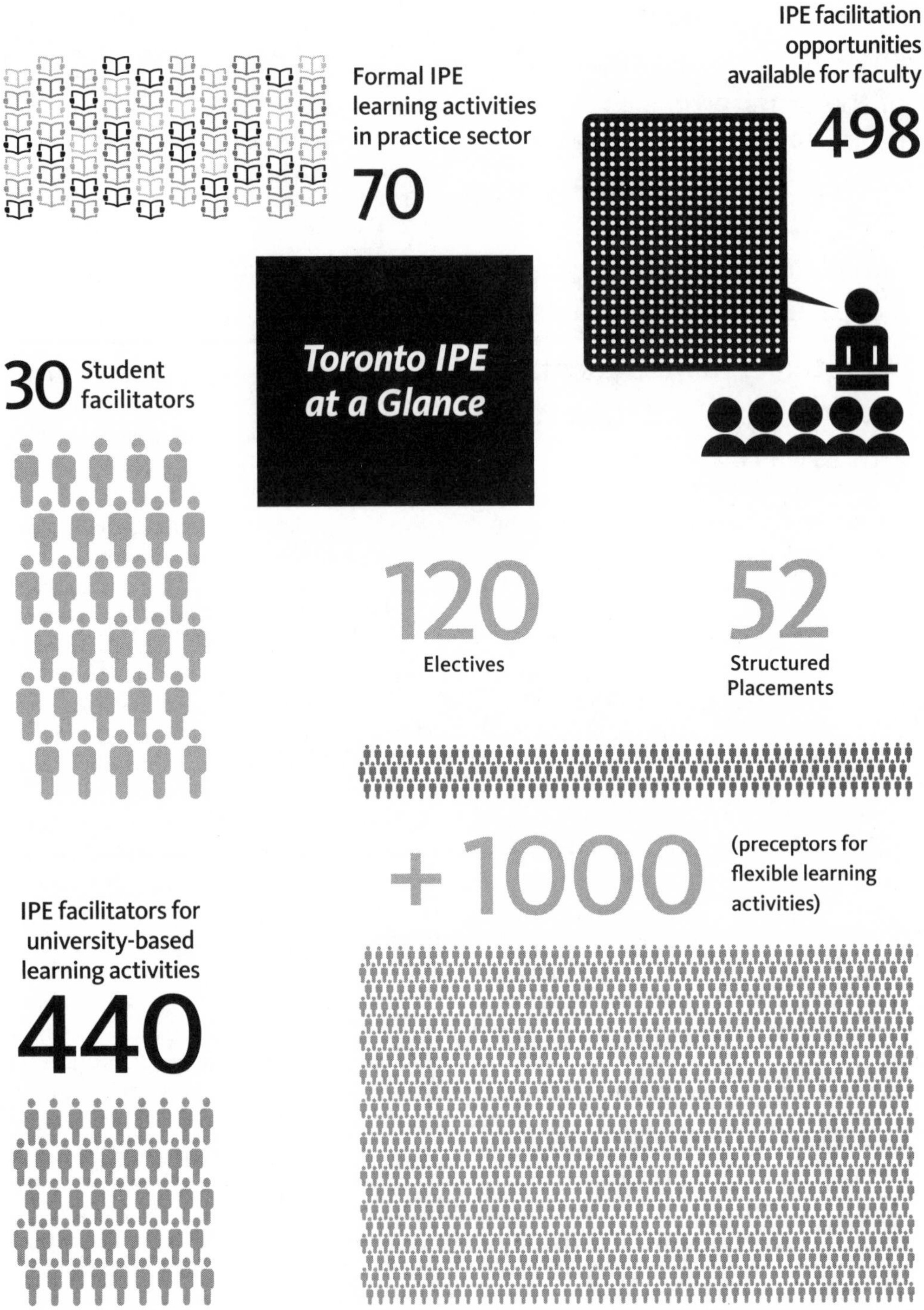

Formal IPE learning activities in practice sector
70

IPE facilitation opportunities available for faculty
498

30 Student facilitators

Toronto IPE at a Glance

120 Electives

52 Structured Placements

IPE facilitators for university-based learning activities
440

+1000 (preceptors for flexible learning activities)

Figure 5—IPE annual participation data

"Pharmacy students need to know the unique strengths of the other professionals they will be working with upon graduation. With the increasing complexities of patient care and the need for more potent medications, the opportunity for detrimental and potentially life-threatening effects has increased."

– K. Wayne Hindmarsh, Canadian Council for Accreditation of Pharmacy Programs

health teams or pain teams, as part of their clinical training. None of those approaches equates with IPE. Inter-professional education is something quite different. It directly addresses the issue of professional culture and identity and looks for ways to assist learners to grow and mature as health professionals (nurses, doctors, pharmacists, and so forth), as well as learning about what their colleagues do and know. It also helps them to develop the skills and capacities to work together to improve care.

Learning how to collaborate with colleagues is not the same as learning with colleagues. If we want practice to be team based, we have to do more than put people into teams. We have to teach people how to collaborate. Importantly, IPE needs to address tenacious issues such as culture, tradition, and power. This is not a task for the faint-hearted.

By the 1980s, in several sites around the world, most notably in the United Kingdom, the idea of interprofessional care had begun to take hold. Studies published in the groundbreaking *Journal of Interprofessional Care* began to pique the interest of Canadian health care leaders. Emeritus Dean of Nursing Dorothy Pringle at the U of T recalls that in the mid-1990s, a Council of Health Sciences Deans was created at the suggestion of the provost, which she subsequently chaired. Pringle remembers that although there was a growing number of initiatives that provided IPE learning opportunities for students at U of T—such as the Year 1 session that brought all first-year students together to attend a panel of patients and clinicians each year—the one thing that everyone felt was missing was practice-based experience in team work. The Council didn't want IPE to be merely a classroom exercise and hit upon the idea that they would use the recently created medical academies, which were academic footholds in the teaching hospitals, as structures around which to build IPE. The ambitious goal of the time was to offer a handful of students from the different programs an opportunity to work with a strong team in a position to model collaborative practice.

Money was found to hire four interprofessional practice coordinators in each of the medical academies to look for great teams suitable for student placement, to work with and

across the different faculty programs to figure out what the curriculum and timetable issues were, and then to work with students during their placements. The whole thing was an experiment in seeing what could be done to bridge the faculties and the hospitals and to support the students in the practice placement. These co-ordinators reported to the Council of Health Sciences Deans and laid the groundwork for the more ambitious scheme that would follow when the timing was right.

> "As with getting most things off the ground, you have to find a few individuals who have a bit of clout."
>
> – Mark Rochon, Associate with KPMG's Global Center of Excellence for Health

In 2000, when the American Institute of Medicine released *To Err Is Human*,[3] the report gave the Canadian interprofessional movement a big push forward. The public revelation that medical errors were killing thousands of patients every year galvanised support for change—not only in the United States but also in Canada.

POLICY DRIVERS

In Canada, the government agenda was also influenced by the 2002 release of *Building on Values: The Future of Health Care in Canada*. In this report, lead author Roy Romanow, a former provincial premier, recommended an integrated approach to preparing health care teams: "If health care professionals are expected to work in teams … their education must prepare them to do so." The Romanow Report made forty-seven recommendations for sweeping changes. Recommendation #17 began: "The Health Council of Canada should review existing education and training programs and provide recommendations to the provinces and territories on more integrated education programs for preparing health care providers."[4]

The Romanow Report led to a series of national and provincial initiatives to support team care, and some U of T leaders were ready to be part of the first charge. One of the great champions of IPE was the Toronto Rehabilitation Institute (Toronto Rehab; now part of University Health Network). The teaching hospital hired Lynne Sinclair, who was in a leadership role at U of T's Department of Physical Therapy, to start up the facility's IPE program and create a sustainable interprofessional learning environment. Sinclair credits the chief nurse executive at the time, Karima Velji, with the vision to appoint her to the city's first IPE job in the practice setting. Sinclair says Velji just "got it" right from the beginning. The stars were aligning for IPE/C in the province of Ontario. Col-

laborative health care delivery had become a political mandate. A handful of champions had by now assembled at U of T and were eager to catch the political wave and move the IPE agenda forward.

How It began

A key early driver at U of T was the establishment of the Office of Interprofessional Education (Office of IPE) under the leadership of founding Director Ivy Oandasan, a family physician. Established in 2005, it would eventually evolve into the Centre for Interprofessional Education (Centre for IPE), described below, in 2009. But in these early years, the foundational work of Oandasan and the Office of IPE concentrated, for the first time, IPE/C efforts in one conceptual and also physical home. Between 2005 and 2009, the Office of IPE played a leading role attaining grants totaling over $17 million by leveraging faculty and health professionals across the university and teaching hospitals. This was enabled by the emergence of both a national and provincial strategy to support team practice in health care and funding incentives in the field. In 2005, Joshua Tepper, a family physician, became Canada's first assistant deputy minister with a health human resources portfolio. To address the shortage of health care workers in Ontario, he believed the province needed more than just additional health professionals. "I knew we had to do things differently," he says. "Health care providers simply had to work differently."

Tepper was a proponent of IPE long before the acronym was coined. His training and early clinical practice in rural, remote settings taught him that each health profession offers unique insights. "The person who taught me how to put on casting was an X-ray technician in Red Lake, Ontario. Her name was Tutsi," he recalls. "The person who taught me how to start IVs was a nurse in Bella Bella, British Columbia. In the U.S., I was taught by physician assistants. Many of my first deliveries were with a midwife in Africa." While Tepper learned to appreciate the knowledge and skills of his colleagues, he doesn't confuse this collegiality with interprofessional care. He explains, "Many people will say, 'Oh, I work on a team because there's

> "In health care settings, we need to change the day-to-day structures that segregate the professions. We need to break down the physical barriers as well as other boundaries, such as scheduling. We need to put mechanisms in place so health care professionals can come together at the point of care."
>
> – Karima Velji, Canadian Nurses Association

a nurse there and a physiotherapist here, and a social worker and doctor over there.' Just because they're all on the same ward doesn't mean you have a team. What you have is a bunch of individuals working in parallel."

The public wasn't as enamored with interprofessionalism as Tepper. "People said the government wanted interprofessional care because it was the cheap way," he recalls. "That's a myth! It is far from a cheap way; in fact, it is probably more expensive. It took time for people to see that this way of delivering care would improve quality because it allows you to leverage a variety of skill sets."

> "Unless you instill in the next generation a commitment and expectation that collaboration is normal and will be accomplished, it can never be accomplished. We have to believe in interprofessionalism for it to become possible."
>
> – Sioban Nelson, Nursing at U of T

Tepper was eventually successful in pushing the IPE/C and quality care agenda in Ontario. IPE proponents at U of T were quick to apply for government dollars at both provincial and national levels, and an opportunity arose in 2005 when Health Canada, the federal government's health department, announced a competition for innovative, potentially transformative projects in IPE/C. Catharine Whiteside, then the Faculty of Medicine's associate dean of Graduate and Inter-faculty Affairs, and Brian Hodges, the second director of the Wilson Centre, were part of the group who came up with a plan for U of T, which at the time had little experience applying for large-scale platform funding for IPE/C. "We stayed up late one night in Catharine's office submitting the final proposal to Health Canada," recalls Hodges. "It was dark, and I remember being very tired. It wasn't perfect, but in the end we decided to give it a shot and submit it."

"There was variable enthusiasm from the other deans," recalls Whiteside. "The reason was that at the time there was little solid evidence that IPE curriculum would lead to better care."

The proposal marked the first collaboration of all of the teaching hospitals and university health faculties. "We had a huge committee, and it was the initial big platform project with everyone's blessing," says Hodges. Although every health faculty and teaching hospital agreed to the proposal, some signed off reluctantly.

"It was hard work to get all the hospitals to agree to the IPE proposal," adds Hodges. "We were trying to make arguments from the emerging literature that interprofessionalism had an impact on patient care, but lots of our colleagues were not that

convinced it was worth doing." Some practitioners questioned whether interprofessional care was a new term for something they were already doing. Others claimed it was just the flavour of the month.

The proposal, submitted just hours before the deadline, was accepted and eventually led to the Structuring Communication Relationships for Interprofessional Teamwork (SCRIPT) program. This three-year research study funded by Health Canada and led by IPE champions Ivy Oandasan (family medicine), Lynne Sinclair (rehabilitation), and Merrick Zwarenstein (general internal medicine) examined how IPE/C could look in different contexts: primary care, rehabilitation, and general internal medicine. SCRIPT's ultimate goal was to transform the conduct, learning, and evaluation of interprofessional teamwork in the teaching hospitals by advancing the evidence base for IPE.

According to Sinclair, the SCRIPT project pulled together an interprofessional team that included rhetorician and qualitative researcher Lorelei Lingard, social scientist Scott Reeves, and nursing and pharmacy faculty Diane Doran and Zubin Austin, respectively, to support collaborative research in the area of IPE/C. Sinclair recalls it as an exciting and energized time when a broad team of colleagues strove to figure out how to work together within and across professions and across contexts and to build the evidence base for IPE/C.

Evidence that IPE would lead to better care was crucial to securing support. Oandasan notes that evidence was building in the early 2000s, including the Health Canada projects described above, her own two major literature reviews, and an environmental scan on IPE/IPC funded by and for Health Canada and the Canadian Health Services Research Foundation in 2004–2005.[5] These projects created seminal documents that are now used internationally to advance interprofessional education and care and to try to establish the links between IPE and IPC. But despite emerging evidence, a common refrain, according to Hodges, was "Where are the data on the efficacy of IPE?" "Linking IPE to hard clinical outcomes remains a challenge—it is difficult to show that patients get better or live longer because of interprofessional education. There are so many factors involved in a patient's recovery that pulling out the variance attributable to IPE is a challenge. Yet, to make such major investments in changing the system, health care leaders want to see evidence."

Faced with a paucity of hard evidence about patient outcomes, in the words of Mark Rochon, founding president and CEO of Toronto Rehab (which in 2006 developed and piloted the first structured IPE placement in Toronto), "It became a

question of commitment and belief... we went down this path based on belief."

Team practice is not in itself new, and some disciplines, such as psychiatry, have long lent themselves to this approach. But what makes for effective team practice? How do we ensure that it isn't hit-and-miss and personality driven? Is getting on well together the same as good team practice? Despite most practitioners declaring themselves strong team players, many health care practitioners are not team-driven. To practice interprofessionally, they have to make a fundamental philosophical shift. "We shouldn't kid ourselves," says Tepper. "We are asking for a very pervasive change, and change is always hard. We are asking people to change how they structure their days, who they talk to and how they talk to them, and how they chart. Time is always a scarce resource for health practitioners, and we are asking them to allocate time to allow an interplay of the members of the team."

When care is interprofessional, the hierarchy is flattened. Any health care practitioner still on a pedestal must step down graciously and collectively problem-solve, share care, and make decisions not only with the other members of the health care team but also with the patient and family. "Interprofessional care requires the courage to step back and say you don't know, and the humility to admit you need help from the team," says Maria Tassone, a physiotherapist and the first director of the Centre for Interprofessional Education, a formal partnership of the U of T and TAHSN, with the University Health Network as the lead hospital. "Since many health care professionals have traditionally been socialized to have the answers themselves, IPE really challenges people to their level of comfort and discomfort."

Around the same time as interprofessionalism was being touted in clinical settings, the government was passing new regulations that increased the overlap in the health professions' scope of practice—notably for nurse practitioners, pharmacists, and physiotherapists. This overlap increased possibilities for collaboration, but it worried some practitioners because now someone else could do part of *their* job.

Power dynamics and the power struggles that result from them are inherent challenges that must be confronted by those who want to introduce interprofessional care and

"Being part of my health care team gave me confidence in my care and in my right as a patient to play an active role in my care, and it respects my input and that of my loved ones."

– Patient Mentor

http://www.health
forceontario.ca/
UserFiles/file/
Policymakers
Researchers/
ipc-blueprint-
july-2007-en.pdf

practice. "The friction, the rub, often came from the discipline leaders. It was a question of authority and control," says Rochon. "You're dividing responsibility and budgets."

"In the end what are we arguing about?" Tepper asks. "We have to realize there's more than enough work for everyone." The former deputy minister's own leadership in this area included creating a provincial platform for IPC and IPE that led to the development of Ontario's *Interprofessional Care: A Blueprint for Action in Ontario.*[6] The Blueprint contained recommendations for regulatory practice changes that ultimately appeared in the Province of Ontario Bill 179, which set the framework for changes to scope of practice to support team-based health care. Tepper's ability to use the provincial government platform to bring together regulators, associations, deans, insurers, and CEOs was a key contextual factor in moving beyond "belief" in IPC to implementation. Once the provincial government was encouraging health system leaders and enabling it through legislation, IPE/C was transformed into a cornerstone of Health Human Resources (HHR) planning in the province.

Whiteside recognized that to successfully introduce IPC and end the turf wars, she first needed to teach the teachers. "If you really want to start something new, you have to start with training and engaging the faculty," she says. "In the Faculty of Medicine at the University of Toronto alone, we have seven thousand faculty members, so it isn't easy, but it is critical."

But knowing what needs to be done and figuring out how to make such major change are two very different things. Whatever the students were being taught in the classrooms, during their clinical placements they could witness a health professional barking orders or see providers brushing off each other's input. "What is modeled in practice can undo what you've taught in the classroom," warns Hodges. "The hidden curriculum is very powerful."

To further interprofessionalism in education, Hodges was part of the group of educators who pushed for collaborative skills to be assessed in medical licensure and certification evaluations though the Royal College of Physicians and Surgeons of

"Our mission as social workers is to work with individuals and their environment in the whole ecological context. We have to be aware of all aspects of the person – his physical health, his emotional health, his family, his community, his school. Interprofessional care ensures that all of the different professions are involved and see the person holistically."

– Faye Mishna, the dean of Social Work at U of T

Canada, the Medical Council of Canada, and the Ontario International Medical Graduate Program. "As soon as you put something in an exam or on an evaluative form, it has a lot more currency with the students," he says. "The students realize it's serious and rise to the occasion. Teachers realize they have to teach it. By the end of the 90s, we had started to evaluate interprofessional care. The exams introduced a competence called 'collaborator' that needed to be assessed. That was a big change for medicine."

The former dean of nursing and now Vice-Provost Academic Sioban Nelson argues that, in comparison to medical education, nursing education is not so strongly structured around accreditation, standardized testing, or simulations. While collaboration is part of the nursing accreditation framework, clearer expectations need to come from the regulators for the schools to really make IPE a major priority. That change has already happened in pharmacy according to Dean Emeritus Wayne Hindmarsh who says "the drive in pharmacy is truly collaborative in nature, from practitioners, regulatory bodies, and educators. We are fortunate that we have interprofessional requirements in our new University and College [for Technicians] standards. It is required!" For the other regulated professions across the country, there is much variation between jurisdictions and professions. The push to adopt more interprofessionally focused education has in some instances come from regulators; in others, it is the educators, leaders in the practice setting, and government that are pushing it forward. In-training assessment forma and in competency frameworks drove the IPE agenda. "To really understand how to engage in IPC, it had to be part and parcel of the teaching," emphasized Whiteside.

Supporting the scholarship of IPE in Toronto was the Wilson Centre for Research in Education. Placing an educational research centre inside a teaching hospital—particularly one promoting an interprofessional approach to research to advance the strong education–practice partnership in Toronto— was a strategic move. Fifteen years on, every U of T extradepartmental unit focused on education, including the Centre for IPE, is now situated in a major teaching hospital. Established in 1997 through an innovative partnership between U of T's Faculty of Medicine and Toronto General Hospital (part of the University Health Network), the Wilson Centre is now one of the largest centres for health profession education research in the world. It replaced the university's Division of Student Medical Education, which, without a central office, had dispersed across campus. "The Wilson Centre needed the cachet of a physical centre," insisted Richard Reznick, a surgeon and

the Centre's founding director and vice president of Education at the University Health Network at the time: "We needed to repatriate the diaspora and give them a home. We needed a physical presence."[7] "The location of the Wilson Centre inside a hospital is unique in the world," points out Hodges. "All of the other centres that research health profession education are in universities." In fact, Reznick insisted that the Wilson Centre not only be in the hospital but in a prominent place in the hospital: "It's on the first floor, in a central location. It's prime real estate," he says proudly. Patients, though, kept wandering into the Wilson Centre looking for the X-ray room or asking what floor the cafeteria is on. Reznick considered the patient traffic an advantage. He would tell the researchers, "The reason you're here is to make patients better. The patients coming and going is a touchstone for why you're here." Reznick was so determined that the Wilson Centre be part of the hospital hub that when the administrators embarked on a renovation and presented a plan to put the Wilson Centre in the basement, Reznick threatened to resign.

When Hodges became the director of the Wilson Centre in 2002, he began to recruit researchers from different disciplines. "We started to get much more cross-pollination," he says, adding that the Wilson Centre now includes sociologists, anthropologists, psychologists, kinesiologists, educationalists, and many other disciplines. Together, the research team began to accumulate critical evidence on the efficacy of interprofessionalism.

One of the Wilson Centre researchers was Lorelei Lingard, a linguistics expert and qualitative researcher. She researched how clinical teams in the operating room (OR) use language and how their communication patterns influence patient safety. After scrubbing up and donning a gown and mask, the rhetorician circulated in the periphery of the OR, observing and scribbling notes. She began to note near-misses and errors that could be directly attributed to failed communication. She grew to understand that communication on clinical teams isn't as simple as people talking to each other. Influencing the information flow are power differentials and the simple fact that some people speak up more than others.[8]

Lingard's research led to the development of the Surgical Safety Checklist, now used around the globe.[9] "The checklist is a series of steps the OR team goes through before they start an operation," explains Hodges. "Each member of the team introduces him- or herself because they don't always know each other. Everybody has an opportunity to say what they need to say. The hierarchy can't interfere with people expressing important information." Hodges recalled a proud moment

when, a few short years later as he was wheeled into the OR for surgery after his appendix had ruptured, the nurse said, "Now we're going through the Surgical Safety Checklist that came from the Wilson Centre."

As momentum continued to build for IPE/C at U of T, support was garnered for the recruitment of a leading international expert in IPE. Sociologist Scott Reeves was recruited to the team. His role was to gather and develop evidence about IPE effectiveness to build the case for IPE expansion both locally at U of T and for health professional education more generally. Reeves, who now leads the Center for Innovation in Interprofessional Education, University of California, San Francisco, was initially appointed in 2005 in a combined move between the Department of Family and Community Medicine and the Wilson Centre, and later appointed at the Centre for Faculty Development and the Li Ka Shing Knowledge Institute at St. Michael's Hospital. He became a core member to the IPE/C team at Toronto.

Based on the successful partnership between the University of Toronto and the teaching hospitals, the Centre for Interprofessional Education was established in 2009 at the University Health Network (Toronto Western site); it replicated many of the features of the Wilson Centre as a unit dedicated to education located in a teaching hospital. The Centre was jointly funded by the University of Toronto, University Health Network, and the Toronto Rehabilitation Institute. This shared financial model resulted from the leadership of surgeon Richard Reznick, who promoted the idea of establishing hard funding that would create a sustainable extradepartmental unit, shared between the U of T and its hospital partners, using the model of the Wilson Centre. Reznick, Sinclair, and Tassone went on the road over the span of four months and met with every TAHSN CEO to discuss how creating a Centre for IPE would provide value to the Toronto community. This building of partnerships and creating the need and energy for the creation of the Centre was a big step in the successful passing of the proposal to develop the Centre for IPE.

> "For years, dentists in private practice have been working interprofessionally with dental assistants, dental hygienists and nurses. But now the population is more complex, and there's more of a need to also work with physicians and pharmacists in particular."
>
> – Daniel Haas, the dean of Dentistry at U of T

The case for the Centre for IPE was enhanced by the remarkable success of the Office of IPE, which had brought the hospitals and the university together to support several IPE initiatives and grants, including the Catalyzing and Sustaining Communities of Collaboration around Interprofessional Care Grant, a $3.4 million project that illustrated what the hospitals and university could do jointly to support IPE/IPC. By 2006, the work of the early IPE proponents had won over more deans and chairs of several health science faculties who endorsed the development of a requisite IPE curriculum. A Provostial Award supported the Office of IPE to develop a new requisite curriculum that would build on existing exemplars such as the pioneering pain curriculum (see below) and on other smaller curricular IPE pieces across the campus. One of the most helpful components that made this agreeable was an environmental scan led by the Office of IPE and conducted by health sciences students in the summer of 2006, showing that faculties and departments were already engaged in many IPE learning activities.

But back in 2003, U of T had made an important first step into the IPE waters by offering students in several health faculties a mandatory one-week program on pain. Since then, with strong leadership from the faculties of nursing, dentistry, pharmacy, and medicine (including the programs of occupational therapy and physical therapy), close to nine hundred students have assembled each year for lectures and small case-based interprofessional groups. Professor Emeritus Judy Watt-Watson, Faculty of Nursing, recalls that at the beginning, an IPE mandatory interprofessional pain curriculum would not have been possible without the support of the deans of the faculties involved and the Centre for the Study of Pain.

These early gains were critical enablers to the creation of a new, more extensive and integrated curriculum. By 2008, such was the support for IPE and the credibility of earlier initiatives that an integrated, university-wide curriculum was endorsed by the health sciences deans and rolled out in 2009 by the Centre for IPE.

Putting in place the initial and critical pieces of such a large-scale curriculum effort fell to Oandasan.

> "At UHN, we recognize that interprofessional education and care goes across everything the organization is trying to accomplish. The opportunity for IPE is the fact that we are a teaching hospital training the values in the people who are going to be recruited here and the next generation of care providers."
>
> – Bob Bell, President and CEO, University Health Network

She led the development of the first Interfaculty Curriculum Committee and catalyzed the partnership with the teaching hospitals. As noted above, this process was facilitated by strong grant support—totaling over $17 million in funding—that flowed from both provincial and national sources between 2006 and 2009.[10] Though the grant funding was plentiful, the Office of IPE was lean, staffed only by Oandasan and an administrative assistant, both supported by the Provostial Award. Nevertheless, under Oandasan's leadership, it became the hub from which the best of what was already happening in IPE and IPC could be shared and the driver of innovative new projects (such as the award-winning *ehpic*™ course described below) that would illustrate the potential of IPE/C.

> "Shared common visions manifested in the willingness of my team to talk with me and each other, allowed us to negotiate goals and treatments realistic to their scope of practice."
>
> – Patient Mentor

By 2009, momentum had built to create more formal structured partnerships between the teaching hospitals and the University, and the U of T Centre for Interprofessional Education was born. The new Centre for IPE would coordinate and promote IPE programs across the university and in clinical placements in Toronto and beyond. Importantly, it was not just a university centre, it was a university–hospital centre. "A really unique aspect of the U of T program is the true partnership and integration between the practice sector and the university sector," says Maria Tassone, who became the Centre for IPE's inaugural director in 2009. "We are the first university, to our knowledge, to say we're not going to develop an IPE curriculum just within the walls of the university; it has to be a partnership with the practice community. From our governance committees to our bilateral funding, to how curriculum is developed, to who shows up for our professional and faculty development activities, it's a fairly equal balance between educators and clinicians. One of the smartest things that Ivy Oandasan did was to engage the clinical community early on."

It was Tassone's job to sort out what it meant to go from the Office of IPE to the Centre for IPE. "The Centre to me represents the very first formal mandate of the university and the hospitals working together," she says. "I consider our role not just interprofessional education, but fostering interprofessional care in the practice community."

In 2011, the U of T Centre for IPE moved from its makeshift office over a drugstore to its own custom-designed space

at Toronto Western Hospital, made possible by the generosity of a donor. The Kalmar family, wanting to make a difference in the lives of patients and families, understood how integrated care would not only enhance services but improve patients' prognoses. "Without the gift, we would not have the sense of permanency we have now," says Tassone. "For the broader community, this physical space on the first floor of the hospital was considered prime real estate. It is a powerful symbol that we've come, we've arrived, we have permanency; interprofessionalism is something real."

Tassone is now focused on building capacity and sustainability for the Centre. "The Centre's earliest contribution was to take work that was piloted and scale it up," she says. The Centre's role was to take the successes of the Office of IPE and to make them mainstream; to build on the curriculum structures that had been put in place in lead hospitals; and to expand activities to meet the needs of 3,700 learners. Since 2009, the Centre spearheaded the tripling of IPE learning opportunities for students, who are offered everything from quick lunch-and-learn sessions to six-week online programs. To meet demand, the Centre is on track to double the learning opportunities by 2015. Demand continues to grow for many of the programs created by the teams led by Oandasan and Tassone. In 2005, Oandasan with key faculty from University of Toronto developed a faculty development course entitled Educating Health Professionals in Interprofessional Care (*ehpic*™). This five-day certificate course for health professionals, educators, and leaders has graduated over nine hundred participants worldwide. It has been implemented in two-, three-, and five-day versions across Canada, the United States, Denmark, Singapore, Australia, and Saudi Arabia. In 2009, Oandasan, Tassone, and other faculty, recognizing the need to build sustainability and equip people with the key leadership skills to catalyze system change, introduced the Collaborative Change Leadership program, a certificate program for health care and health education leaders originally funded jointly by the Ministry of Health and Long-Term Care's Interprofessional Education and Care Fund. The *ehpic*™ course and the Collaborative Change Leadership program have attracted so much international attention that they both have waiting lists filled with health care and health education leaders eager to attend.

Students are a key ingredient in the Centre's success. While faculty across hospitals and universities created IPE learning opportunities, students became engaged as mentors and teachers. The National Health Sciences Students' Association (NaHSSA), formed in 2005, is the first and only national

interprofessional student association in the world. The University of Toronto chapter, Interprofessional Healthcare Students' Association (IPHSA), champion IPE and IPC activities within their faculties. It has not only helped develop curriculum by participating in curriculum working groups but also created its own IPE electives. For the past three years, IPHSA initiated a large-scale survey of all health science students to determine what is working well within the IPE curriculum and where things needs to grow and evolve. This work shaped a number of changes to programming and the infrastructure available for IPE. The student group has supported a number of interprofessional social events to connect students outside of formal curricular time—an important element in building team effectiveness in any context.

Interprofessionalism at Toronto, while now close to being a mainstream concept, is still young. Much needs to be done, and much of what needs doing involves system changes. But there's also much to be celebrated. "The most fundamental shift has been that people no longer ask, 'Why should we do IPE?' Now, they ask, 'How do we do it? How do we go from good to great?'" says Tepper. "Within a decade, I think that's pretty awesome!"

Reflection Questions: Getting Started

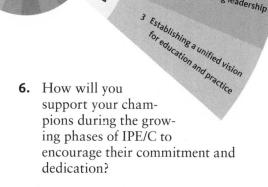

1 The importance of champions

2 Engaging leadership

3 Establishing a unified vision for education and practice

CHAPTER 1

THESE REFLECTION QUESTIONS provide a starting point for those interested in getting the ball rolling and building a team of IPE/C champions at their institution.

1. Where is IPE and IPC already living in your practice and academic settings? Where is there energy for IPE/C that you might leverage... in the education, practice, regulatory, accreditation, and/or legislative systems?

2. What are the priorities in your settings and systems that IPE/C might enable (e.g., quality, safety, patient-centered care)?

3. What exemplars currently exist—locally, regionally, nationally, or internationally—that could be used and shared as success stories from which to build?

4. What can be learned from others' successes?

5. The role of champions is critical. Who are your "storm chasers"? How might you connect with and support them?

6. How will you support your champions during the growing phases of IPE/C to encourage their commitment and dedication?

7. Are there colleagues doing interprofessional work whose insights and knowledge could be tapped?

8. What might be possible by building and growing an IPE/C program that isn't possible now?

9. What difference could be made for students, faculty, patients, families, and the health care system through your IPE/C program?

10. What opportunities exist through innovative funding to bring researchers, academics, and clinicians together to develop IPE/C both in the classroom and in clinical settings?

11. What are the drivers for advancing IPE and IPC in your contexts?

CHAPTER 2

Structuring for Success

LAYING THE FOUNDATION

EACH UNIVERSITY AND TEACHING HOSPITAL HAS ITS OWN UNIQUE structure and organization. A successful IPE/C program needs to take advantage of whatever structures and forums exist in an organization and to build on these to start the discussion, mobilize support, and develop a sustainable plan. At the University of Toronto (U of T), that forum was the Council of Health Sciences.

At the U of T, there are five single-department health faculties (dentistry, kinesiology and physical education, nursing, pharmacy, and social work), and one multidepartmental faculty, medicine, that houses a further six professional programs: medical radiation sciences, occupational science and occupational therapy, physical therapy, physician assistant program, speech language pathology, and undergraduate medicine. The deans and chairs of the health science faculties come together at the Council of Health Sciences, a forum that represents the health professional programs. It was at this forum that the proposal to establish an IPE curriculum first emerged in 2005 and received full support from the health sciences leadership in an application to the provost to fund the initiative. This formal leadership of the deans and chairs (along with provostial support) legitimized the establishment of IPE and established the mandate to create the space within each health professional program for IPE content and activities. Each faculty council approved the curriculum. The engagement and leadership by faculty members enabled each program to be designed and implemented in a way that complemented each program's uniprofessional curriculum.

HIGHLIGHTS

1 Creating a partnership

2 Building enabling structures

3 Creating leaders at all levels

4 How it's paid for

The Council of Health Sciences charged the Interfaculty Curriculum Committee (IFCC), a new and critical structure that was established in 2007, with overseeing and endorsing the development, implementation, and evaluation of the requisite longitudinal IPE Curriculum for the 3,700 students in the health science programs. Prior to its establishment, there was no formal way for curriculum leaders across the health sciences to have dialogue about joint curricular issues. Unlike IPE committees in other universities, which often have membership of "IPE advocates," the IFCC was purposefully constituted through membership recommended by the dean/chair of each program. This decision was made to ensure that those sitting on the IFCC had the power within their own programs to make curriculum decisions. As such, many of the original members of the IFCC had minimal knowledge of IPE and needed to be supported in their learning about the pedagogy associated with it. As a representative committee, originally chaired by the director of the Office of IPE, there is one member appointed by the dean or chair from each of the eleven health science programs. The IFCC provides a critical forum for planning and decision making regarding current and emerging curricular issues, such as development of content in new strategic areas or assessment strategies and methods that will be used across professions to determine how students are meeting IPE competencies.

Susan Wagner (Department of Speech-Language Pathology) was the first Faculty Lead, Curriculum charged with developing the key components for the requisite IPE curriculum from 2007 to 2012. Working with Sylvia Langlois (current Faculty Lead, Curriculum and former IPE Curriculum Associate); Brian Simmons, Faculty Lead, Assessment; and Kathryn Parker, Faculty Lead, Program Evaluation, all worked with the IFCC in the early years to establish the blueprint needed for successful implementation. Wagner recalls the IFCC was uncharted territory: "It didn't come together right away. It took a long time to figure out how to work together" as many of the committee members were knowledgeable about uniprofessional learning needs for their discipline and less on interprofessional learning requirements emerging through upcoming accreditation standards being proposed Canada-wide.

> "We have expectations of people working as teams, but we train them in guilds. How can we expect them to work together? Everyone needs to know what contributions each profession brings to the table."
>
> – Mark Rochon, Associate with KPMG's Global Center of Excellence for Health

One challenge the IFCC had to deal with is that curriculum belongs to each program/department/faculty, which is directly responsible for providing their learners with a curriculum to satisfy the differing lengths of programs, as well as requirements to graduate. Programs may be two, three, or four years in length. Some programs are at the graduate level, others undergraduate. Some programs require students to spend a great deal of time in clinical settings, others much less. But the hardest differences to negotiate were not structural but related to the varying culture and values. To the surprise of many of the original IFCC members, there was a need to develop a common language to make educational decisions. Before they could even get started on the mammoth task of developing a common curriculum, the IFCC members needed to uncover shared values and their vision and purpose for educating U of T health science graduates. Professional cultures were so much stronger than anyone had anticipated.

To develop the requisite IPE curriculum, the IFCC had to step back from the nitty-gritty of the curriculum in which they had become mired and reach higher, adopting a values-based approach to find the necessary common ground. Embarking on a values exercise allowed the committee to see beyond the diversity of their professions/disciplines and to discover common territory for the type of learners they wanted to graduate from U of T's IPE requisite curriculum. They realized that to reach the common goal of creating effective team-based practitioners, learners in all the professions needed a curriculum founded on explicit values shared across disciplines that would enable them to graduate with both uni- and intraprofessional competence. There were many "growing pains," as Wagner coined them, for the IFCC. One particularly frustrating issue concerned the seemingly varying level of commitment from different professional programs; for instance some members attended regularly while others were sporadic. With that unevenness, it was hard to keep everyone's commitment, recalled Wagner. Adjusting to personalities and turnover of members takes its toll when doing difficult and pioneering work. The take-home message from Wagner is that patience is important. "Stick with it," she insists, "it does come together." "It really was about team building—we had to live it. We were crossing the bridge the same time we were building it."

> **"Health care is far too complex to use only the single lens of one profession."**
>
> – Sylvia Langlois, Occupational Science and Occupational Therapy at U of T, faculty lead, Centre for Interprofessional Education at U of T

"In the beginning, interprofessional education was just a term. People had to see it as theirs. They needed to own it. You can't tell anyone what to do. You can only help them uncover what they need to do."

– Ivy Oandasan, Family and Community Medicine at U of T, Inaugural Director Office of Interprofessional Education

Managing tensions between the curricular programs and the Office of IPE was also a challenge. People are very territorial about their curriculum content. While the Office (and now the Centre for IPE) can help to bring the faculties together, decisions are always made by the individual health science programs. Wagner advises that anyone going down this path establish clear parameters concerning roles, responsibilities, and authority as soon as possible.

Ivy Oandasan, founding director of the Office of IPE, further stresses the "importance of the curriculum structure to make decisions—this is what has been missing in many places going down the path of IPE and IPC. Too many have just IPE advocate groups. That is different from having a curriculum decision-making body... This is not a committee on the side. If universities are serious, they need to make this an important structure and give it power to make decisions... Without it, the curriculum will not fly."

Recognition is an important factor. Wagner feels passionate about the need for this work to be recognized within each of the divisions in terms of the workload of faculty members. "This was a hard-working committee that met for 2.5 hours each month for years. It did a lot of groundbreaking work, but not everyone received recognition for it within [their] own programs," says Wagner. Through the advocacy and leadership of the Centre for IPE at the Council of Health Sciences table, she is pleased these roles now bring with them a one day per week workload allocation. "Time is the most valuable resource of all, and unless people's time is recognized the work will never be as important as other activities." The issue of providing support and protected time for individuals charged with IPE/C is an important one and has generated much discussion over the years in Toronto. We discuss in more detail the specific jobs associated with IPE in Chapter 4.

Key successes of the curriculum committee in its early years included the development of the Framework for the Development of Interprofessional Education Values and Core Competencies, now recognized as an international exemplar by the Josiah Macy Jr. Foundation; the Points for Interprofessional Education System (PIPES) framework, which uses both process and content criteria to determine

the quality of existing and/or new IPE learning activities; and the development of global rating scales as a self-assessment methodology for students.

Asked what she would say to others considering developing a common curriculum, Wagner is quick to stress how much fun it is despite the challenges. It worries her that people might not see that. "It's easy to forget how much fun it is to work with smart and creative people on innovative projects." She emphasizes that it has been a wonderful experience all along the way. "It's very rich. You build great links and a wonderful network."

PARTNERING WITH STUDENTS

Toronto students have a parallel structure, the Interprofessional Healthcare Students' Association (IPHSA), an interprofessional forum to promote and advance IPE in their respective programs. The IPE curriculum successes have been in part a result of engagement and collaboration with this student group, which is a local chapter of the National Health Sciences Students' Association (NaHSSA). IPHSA's mandate is to create an educational environment in which students have the opportunity to interact and learn from one another. Student members of IPHSA believe that fostering a strong interprofessional relationship, involving understanding, appreciation, and cooperation among the health professions, is key to providing patients with the best care they can receive. As such, two members of IPHSA have been sitting on the IFCC with voting privileges since 2010. Students are also leading the development of new IPE curricular activities that are meaningful to them, in collaboration with faculty.

Elisa Simpson, a former nursing student and IPHSA co-president, explains: "One of the most important activities that IPHSA does as a student organization includes compiling the student feedback we receive based on our annual IPE student survey and then presenting the results to the Interfaculty Curriculum Committee to ensure that the students' voices are heard."

Nikki Fischer, medicine student and past member of IPHSA executive , adds: "I think one of the most important things, in the past, has been advocacy on behalf of students. Originally IPE was formed from the faculty perspective, without a lot of student involvement, so [our role

> "There's no question: the students see interprofessional education as incredibly relevant to their practice and their careers."
>
> – Maria Tassone, Physical Therapy at U of T, Director of the Centre for Interprofessional Education

has] been a lot about what students value in IPE which has been really valuable for incorporating what students want to see in the curriculum."

IPHSA has taken this task to heart. Its long list of accomplishments include initiating and leading a major survey of students that led to a dramatic increase in electives offered in 2011; successful advocacy for representation on the IFCC; and, in 2010, the launch of their own popular learning activity, an orientation to the various health science professions. It wasn't always easy for IPHSA, however. Oandasan recalls the early struggles of the society and the support it needed from the Office of IPE. Uniprofessional student groups have well-established identities and support structures within their faculties, and interprofessional groups need commitment from the deans and the IPE leaders if they are going to be successful. Recognition, legitimacy, and acceptance took time, support, and committed student leadership. Interprofessional education and practice is about changing the way teams—student teams, teaching teams, and practicing teams—work. It is predicated on the ability to create a different dynamic between colleagues outside of the classroom, in the classroom, and in the practice setting.

THE UNIVERSITY-HOSPITAL STRUCTURE

The hospitals within the Toronto Academic Health Science Network (TAHSN) are deeply engaged in teaching and academic practice. These are all fully independent, publicly funded hospitals with their own governing boards and management; all are strongly connected to the University. Governed by wide-ranging academic affiliation agreements, our university-hospital partnerships are quite different than the university-owned teaching facilities more common in the United States, or the government-sanctioned academic health science centres in the United Kingdom. Rather, TAHSN is a loose consortium of independent service providers linked to the University directly through health professions education and research and cohering around common goals to advance the research and education mission across the health sciences and across the city.

> "Leadership for interprofessional teamwork is crucial. The senior management team of an organization needs to understand that this is a goal that the organization expresses and looks to accomplish in all that it does. It's not another silo of activity."
>
> – Bob Bell, President and CEO, University Health Network

The development of IPE was one such common goal and was quickly embraced by each member hospital.

Responding to both the government of Ontario's articulated priority to build IPE/C in the province and U of T's enthusiasm to champion the development across the university, TAHSN was highly engaged in the development of the IPE curriculum and providing opportunities for learners from the outset. Many organizations also adopted creative approaches to foster professional development of staff to transform practice and build effective teams, at the same time directly addressing such issues as the hidden curriculum and its impact on new models of interprofessional learning for students. Further, many organizations also worked closely with the Office and then Centre for IPE to build supports and education for staff teaching IPE. Staff have longstanding experiences of teaching in practice settings within their own profession, but interprofessional teaching was new to many and required intentional learning and support to ensure rich interprofessional learning opportunities in practice settings.

Canadian hospitals are not-for-profit corporations. As such they are responsible to a board that is, in turn, responsible for the appointment of a senior leader (usually president and CEO), who is actively involved in monitoring hospital strategy and outcomes, including quality. Hospital boards, senior management teams, and hospital executives have placed increasing emphasis on patient-centred care, patient safety, and the promulgation of indicators of quality, often expressed through a "balanced scorecard" reporting system. In recent decades there have been high hopes that a movement toward IPE would lead to better outcomes and, in particular, accelerate the movement toward patient-centred care and patient safety.

Evidence of such a relationship emerged with new team-based tools such as the Surgical Safety Checklist—the University Health Network–developed tool that demonstrated links between team education and reducing mortality in an international eight-hospital study by Alex B. Haynes and colleagues (2009).[1] The evidence is growing, too, on the impact of interprofessional care, team functioning, and improved patient outcome measures. For instance, research by Mollie Marr and colleagues (2012)[2] at a New York trauma center showed that interprofessional team education improves outcomes such as role clarity and decreasing time for critical procedures such as

> "Interprofessional health care teams liberated my limited energies to focus on my recovery, instead of managing it."
>
> – Patient Mentor

intubation during resuscitation. Cardiac surgery teams, too, have found a demonstrated impact on team functioning during a crisis following interprofessional team training (Stevens et al. 2012).[3] Hospitals, therefore, have become increasingly interested in improving patient outcomes across a whole host of services by moving to team-based care. Alan Bleakley and colleagues (2012)[4] found that IPE produced a demonstrable shift in team culture and attitudes toward safety in the operating room. Evidence is mounting that team-based education improves the ability to work in teams, which in turn improves care; the type of education required to achieve these outcomes is IPE. Yet health professional education continues in uniprofessional silos.

In Toronto, several structures evolved that have allowed the interest in IPC and IPE to develop materially in hospitals. First and foremost was the creation of the Centre for IPE. As we have noted, since its establishment in 2009, the Centre has been building from the foundational work of the Office of IPE, a more informal structure created in 2005 to establish IPE as a priority at the University of Toronto that reported to the deans. It led to the three-year curricular development project described above. While the focus of the Office of IPE was primarily on curriculum, the Centre for IPE's mandate expanded to reflect the need to focus its efforts at the interface of education and practice, fostering both IPE and IPC. In the previous chapter we introduced the concept of an extradepartmental unit (EDU). As a joint undertaking between the University of Toronto and the University Health Network, the Centre for IPE (CIPE) is supported and funded jointly by both partners, governed by a joint executive, and reports to both health professional faculty deans and hospital CEOs. Extradepartmental units are unique structures; they typically sit outside the formal boundaries of a department and focus on a theme identified as a strategic priority for the University, TAHSN, and its lead hospitals. Other such EDUs include the Wilson Centre for Research in Education, the Centre for Faculty Development, and the Centre for Patient Safety. The EDU model not only provided a "home base" for the IPE initiatives described above but also, in the case of the Centre for IPE, allowed (though not immediately) the creation of a physical space on hospital terrain that would be the instantiation of a commitment to IPE and IPC.

Toronto teaching hospitals take their education mission very seriously. All have created vice president roles for the education portfolio. VPs

> **"The hospitals have been true partners. They've led the way."**
>
> – Maria Tassone, Physical Therapy at U of T, Director of the Centre for Interprofessional Education

for education are individuals who are part of hospital senior management teams and responsible for overseeing not only medical education but all forms of health professions education, often in collaboration with administrative leads of nursing and other health professions. Whereas a decade ago, oversight and support of educational activities at hospitals followed strictly unidisciplinary lines (a director of medical education, a director of nursing education, a director of

> **"Being treated as a valued member of my team was completely unexpected, and I felt honoured to be treated this way."**
>
> – Patient Mentor

pharmacy education, etc.), today there are many overlapping relationships. For example, many hospitals monitor "learner experience" using tools and metrics that are shared across professions. Some have implemented education development programs for hospital-based teachers that are interprofessional. VPs for education have close relationships with all health professionals and key players (e.g., chief nursing executives, vice presidents of professional affairs) and are involved in hospital-based education and training programs that are increasingly interprofessional.

In addition to this infrastructure on the education side, hospitals have also invested in IPE clinical leaders. These individuals, most of whom have dedicated time in their roles, ensure that clinical IPE activities, such as structured and flexible IPE student placements, are available and coordinated at the hospital level. The creation of these clinical leader roles in eighteen area hospitals over the past few years, a reflection of the strong partnership between the Centre for IPE as a TAHSN resource and hub, has been pivotal to the rapid growth of opportunities for students to learn in real interprofessional practice settings. These roles have also been critical to the growth and expansion of the IPE curriculum over the past three years, reflected in the large number and menu of IPE elective activities that are available for students in the Toronto area hospitals. The Centre has supported the growing network of IPE clinical leads by offering mentorship to these individuals on specific initiatives, to help them adapt, implement, and evaluate structured IPE placements; and by bringing them together as a network of leaders throughout the year to continue to build capacity for IPE in the practice setting. In a similar way, the Centre for IPE also supports a new network of Academic Coordinators of Clinical Education (ACCEs) (those that are responsible for clinical placements within uniprofessional programs). At various times, the ACCEs and IPE clinical leaders come togeth-

er to focus on shared planning of interprofessional learning opportunities in practice.

Along with the network of IPE clinical leaders, the Centre for IPE also supports a robust Interprofessional Community of Practice (CoP) across Toronto. Bringing together practice and education leaders across the city, the CoP evolved out of the Catalyzing and Sustaining Communities of Collaboration around Interprofessional Care project led by Oandasan, which was funded by the provincial government in 2007 through a $3.4 million grant that brought teams of faculty and clinicians together across the university and hospitals to advance IPE/C. This project represented the first time the University had partnered with six of the major teaching hospitals

Funding IPE at Toronto

A common question we receive concerning our IPE curriculum is: How is it paid for? That's a complicated question and an evolving story that we will try to set out as clearly as we can through the following questions.

Who pays for the development and delivery of the courses at the university?

1. All U of T professional programs contribute a portion of the budget to the Centre for IPE to deliver the core curriculum. It is a set amount per incoming student approved annually by the Council of Health Sciences. That funding has to be found within each program's budget. There are no university funds for this beyond the original Provostial Award described earlier.

2. Program-specific leads in IPE receive one day per week time release to recognize their IPE workload. Programs find this funding within existing resources.

3. Individual faculty members develop and teach IPE electives as part of their normal faculty teaching workload. Short (seminar length) electives would be considered the equivalent of a guest lecture. Further, many electives as part of the IPE curriculum are also hosted and led across numerous teaching hospitals as part of the hospital's teaching contributions.

No funding changes hands between faculties for the teaching of students from other faculties.

How is the Centre for IPE funded?

Core funding for the Centre for IPE comes from a grant from the provost to the Council for Health Sciences as well as funding from University Health Network.

to enable new projects that crossed education and practice in key areas, such as interprofessional practice mentorship, preceptorship, leadership, and coaching. The project went on to win the Ted Freedman Award for Innovation in Education in 2009, an award given by the Ontario Hospital Association. Since that time, the CoP meets on a regular basis to continue the momentum and collective work with IPC in Toronto. The development of the CoP was foundational to creating a network of champions who could be supported and energized by their peers. It created a critical place for innovators to meet and a supportive network to build sustainability and capacity. In this way, ideas were shared across centres and adapted and expanded to new contexts.

Private philanthropy supported the development of a dedicated space for the Centre. The Centre is also supported through small revenues from its professional development programs and consulting activities.

How are clinicians funded to participate in IPE activities with students?

For health professionals, mentoring and precepting students and teaching IPE electives within the university or in practice are considered part of their normal professional teaching responsibilities within the teaching hospitals. Many of the individuals involved in these activities are cross-appointed to the University, and this work fits under the umbrella of "academic duties." Over the years, there has been greater willingness by clinical teachers to mentor health professional students outside of their home disciplines. No specific funding is provided, but these activities are reported in annual activity reports, form part of teaching portfolios, and are well regarded in promotion dossiers at the university and in performance reviews within the practice setting.

How are clinicians supported to participate in professional development activities for IPE/C?

All hospitals have invested significant funds to support professional development activities, especially in the area of IPE/C. Professional development activities for IPE range from short sessions on IPE small group facilitation to year-long programs on collaborative leadership. Individuals tend to be supported (fully paid and released from normal work responsibilities) for the longer programs. Shorter sessions may be included in work time or may need to be taken in the staff member's own time. It depends on the hospital as well as the unit or program where the individual works.

Finally, there has been a major shift at the top. Hospital CEOs and vice presidents in Toronto regularly speak about the value and importance of IPE and IPC, conversant in a discourse that would have been unimaginable a decade ago. In 2011 the vice presidents of education from across the teaching hospitals developed a forum—called TAHSN-E—which is co-chaired by one of the VPs of education and the associate vice provost of health professional education at the university. This committee meets to discuss strategic issues across all the teaching sites; develops joint initiatives, such as a common set of key performance indicators or learning platforms, to support student engagement and learning; and works to advance education across the clinical setting for all professions in all the sites. IPE/C is a key issue for this group, and the forum allows for shared learning to advance individual hospital sites, as well as systemwide efficiencies to support IPE and advance knowledge and practice in this area.

IPE/C is now so firmly established among the TAHSN partners that hospital foundations have been supportive of interprofessional projects and innovations. While Toronto still awaits an endowed chair in IPE, this appears as a priority in several hospital fund-raising campaigns.

Reflection Questions:
Structuring for Success

CHAPTER 2

7 How it's paid for
6 Creating leaders at all levels
5 Building enabling structures
4 Creating a partnership

CONSIDER WHAT RESTRUCTURING OF LEADER-
ship, administration, or organizational
charts might be necessary to support a
more interprofessional way of functioning at
your institution.

1. What structures already
   exist that might act as enablers of IPE/C? What else
   needs to be created to bring
   faculty, students, practice
   partners, and/or leaders
   together?

2. Where are decisions currently made for developing
   and implementing learning
   that spans two or more
   professions? What structure
   could be developed to help
   facilitate decision making?

3. Which strategies will
   maximize faculty, student,
   clinician, and leader engagement?

4. Where will the hub and
   spokes of your IPE/C
   program be located? What
   resources (physical, human,
   financial, infrastructure)
   will you need?

5. What are the
   powerful symbols that you
   will draw on to build and
   grow your IPE/C program
   (e.g., integrated education
   space, interprofessional
   awards, and incentives)?

6. What education–practice
   partnerships might you
   nurture?

7. What opportunities could
   be created to build IPE
   learning opportunities in
   the practice environment
   for students and clinicians
   alike?

8. What exists in your context
   to support the sharing of
   innovations and the ability
   to catalyze new ideas and
   new champions? What role
   might a Community of
   Practice have in your system and how might such a
   community be supported?

Building the Curriculum

I N THIS CHAPTER WE LOOK AT THE NUTS AND BOLTS OF INTERPROFES-sional education (IPE)—the curriculum. We are often asked, "How is it possible to harness the enthusiasm of champions and to move from local innovations to an integrated framework that is part of the core experience of all health science students?" The answer to that question rests with the creation of a joint curriculum and the process that exercise initiates. In this chapter we look at the curriculum framework and its multiple components. We discuss its introduction, development, and evolution, but, most important, we look at the process that accompanied this enormous endeavor as the key to successful implementation, continued adaptation, and sustainability.

Following are the key elements of the IPE curriculum discussed in this chapter:

- *Core competencies*—the University of Toronto (U of T) approach
- *Points for Interprofessional Education System (PIPES)* framework for the development of learning activities, both core and elective
- The first three (of four) *core learning activities* that students complete as part of their requisite IPE curriculum
- *Case studies* that provide examples of elective learning activities

The fourth and final core learning activity, the IPE Component in a Clinical Placement, is discussed in Chapter 4 given its crucial role in fostering education-practice partnerships and building capacity of clinical IPE environments.

Creating curriculum is a complex enterprise involving a long series of negotiations. While teachers continually update

HIGHLIGHTS

1 Creating time and space for IPE

2 Fostering engagement

3 Maintaining commitment

4 Overcoming challenges

and revise their course content, adding or removing substantive curriculum content involves major discussion, justification to multiple stakeholders, and progress through many levels of governance. Typical for a North American university, governance at the University of Toronto involves a series of faculty- or department-level committees that includes undergraduate and graduate curriculum committees. Decisions made by these bodies need to be approved at Faculty Council (a form of senate), then progress to Academic Board for approval, and, depending on their extensiveness, from there they may then go forward to the provincial Quality Council that oversees all university programs. Substantial curriculum innovations can take up to two years for final approval. Along the way, faculty, instructors, and students have input into these changes. For health sciences programs public consultation typically involves clinical partners, professional groups, regulators, and accreditors. In the case of IPE curricula, each program must approve the content though its own governance structures in order to meet their individual accreditation standards. This creates a cumbersome process involving a parallel sequence of internal discussions involving professional stakeholders, followed by consultation and review processes that may (eventually) involve other professions.

In light of this complexity, the creation of an interprofessional curriculum is a seriously daunting task that requires diplomacy, strong negotiation skills, and, above all, unflinching resolve. The first question that confronts an enthusiastic team of early adopters who want to revolutionize uniprofessional education (and subsequently patient/client care) and create the high-functioning teams of the future, is how to scale the walls of the silos in which the generation and approval of curriculum takes place.

At U of T, the mechanism adopted to launch IPE from the fringe to the mainstream was the creation of the Interfaculty Curriculum Committee (IFCC) introduced in Chapter 2. This committee is comprised of a designated representative from each of the eleven participating health programs. As part of their oversight mandate for the entire IPE curriculum, this committee is a conduit for the interprofessional curriculum discussions happening across the eleven curricula and the individual program-based curriculum committees.

"It took a long time to find the common place from which we could move forward. The diversity of the programs and the strong sense of culture that everyone brought to the table made it difficult. We had to learn to work together."

– Susan Wagner, Speech Language
   Pathology at U of T, former chair of IFCC

COMPETENCY-BASED IPE

The IFCC's first task was to develop and then approve a curriculum framework for the health science professions at U of T. Although some programs had competency frameworks, and thus competencies, in place, the idea of competency-based education had not fully taken hold across the health sciences. In nursing, for instance, the curriculum had long been based on the national competency framework for nursing, and each program in the country was accredited on that basis. However, the competencies for nursing and medicine, for example, are not similar in structure or content. Other programs, such as kinesiology, have not so far utilized a competency approach; therefore, the idea of an IPE competency framework required familiarization and intense internal discussion.

The challenge was to bring diverse faculties, leaders, and students together and to begin to develop an interprofessional curriculum, using a collaborative and highly engaging approach to creating common competencies across the health sciences. The IFCC had an ongoing mission—to ensure IPE was embedded in the uniprofessional curriculum in a sustainable way, thus institutionalizing IPE as a core curriculum component of U of T health professional programs. Determining core competencies was an essential foundational step for developing a competency-based IPE curriculum at U of T. A working group, led by Susan Wagner as part of her role as Faculty Lead for curriculum, developed the specific competencies, anchored in an overall competency framework, between April 2007 and January 2008. This work was made possible by a grant from the provincial government that funded faculty projects leads. The process involved the exploration and examination of relevant literature, models, and resources, and then brainstorming with the team to create a Toronto approach to interprofessional core competencies.

The final product of these deliberations was a core competency framework created to encompass a learning continuum from pre–health science programs to U of T health professional programs to postgraduation. The end goal was

> "Multidisciplinary care was what we did when we were thrown together. Multidisciplinary care wasn't reflected on; interprofessional care is. Interprofessional care is a more deliberate and considered way of thinking about all the different contributions of people in health care and how those contributions can be integrated to maximize what is possible."
>
> – Charmaine Williams, Social Work at U of T

interprofessional collaborative practice, and the competency framework provided the pathway for the learner to become a skilled member of a patient/client-focused team providing a collaborative approach to care. In 2008, U of T's former Office of IPE published this framework and the accompanying thirty essential competencies (see Figure 7). This chart not only informed IPE programs at the university, but subsequently contributed to Canada's national interprofessional competency framework and several other frameworks across North America. The University of Toronto's IPE curriculum and framework built on the pioneering work done during the same period across the country, especially at the University of British Columbia, including the triadic concept of "exposure, immersion, and mastery."[1]

"There's a lot of overlap in the competencies set out by the various organizations, but everyone seems to love their own framework," says Maria Tassone, director of the Centre for IPE. "What I like about U of T's framework is that it elevates and makes explicit the values and ethics components of interprofessional education." One of the values is creativity/innovation, which Tassone says calls for imaginative ways of practicing. "Health care and health care teams are constantly changing and adapting, so it involves a fair bit of improvisation. We need to think more about improv as a pedagogical strategy in the curriculum."

The IPE curriculum is anchored around three constructs articulated in U of T's Framework for the Development of Interprofessional Education Values and Core Competencies: (1) Collaboration, (2) Communication and (3) Values and Ethics (see Figure 6). The first of the three constructs, Values

Figure 6— The Framework for the Development of Interprofessional Education Values and Core Competencies

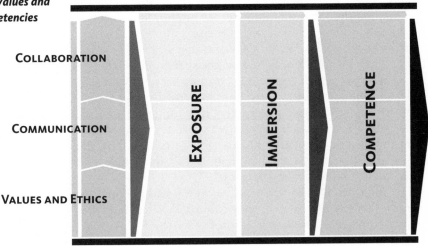

and Ethics, focuses heavily on relationships with the health care team (relational-centred care), including patient/client to practitioner, practitioner to practitioner, practitioner to community, and practitioner to self. Within the Communication construct, students are engaged in IPE learning activities focused on listening, navigating conflict, effective communication, and giving and receiving feedback. Finally, Collaboration introduces interprofessional (IP) theory, and explores roles and responsibilities within the IP health care team. Students also have the opportunity to engage in activities focused on change and self-reflection. Each of these constructs runs longitudinally through the phases of Exposure (introduction), Immersion (development), and Competence (entry to practice). Underlying all of this is a process of continual reflection, learning, and formative assessment. The competency framework acknowledges that students arrive in their respective health science programs with their own personal values and competencies shaped by their unique experiences. From here, the IPE curriculum is introduced early to integrate and instill interprofessional values and competencies that leverage the students' uniprofessional learning. Postgraduation, students continue as lifelong learners to master IPE concepts and competencies through practice experience, graduate studies, and/ or continuing education. In the journey toward mastery, practitioners are encouraged and enabled to engage in IPE teaching and facilitation opportunities within the academic and/or practice environments.

ASSESSMENT OF CORE COMPETENCIES

Each learning activity within the IPE curriculum includes pre- and postlearning activity self-assessments (measured by global rating scales) completed by the students. These provide a five-point anchored Likert scale for each of the core competencies (from the Values and Ethics, Communication, and Collaboration constructs). Students provide an assessment of their perceived learning before and after each learning experience.

"Since I have been a mentor I have come across former students who have spoken to me about how our conversations have influenced them in the way they deal with patients."

– Health Mentor

THE FOUR CORE LEARNING ACTIVITIES

Teamwork: Your Future in Interprofessional Health Care

Case-Based Session – either Pain or Palliative Care

Conflict in Interprofessional Life

IPE Component in a Clinical Placement

A FRAMEWORK FOR THE DEVELOPMENT OF INTERPROFESSIONAL EDUCATION VALUES

EXPOSURE: INTRODUCTION

CONSTRUCTS

ENTRY-LEVEL ASSESSMENT

Collaboration

- Interprofessional (IP) theory
- Context and culture of the health care system
- Roles, responsibilities, accountabilities, and scope of practice
- Decision making/ critical thinking
  - Perform as an effective team member
    - Flexibility, cooperation, contribution, organization/efficiency, team health maintenance
- Self-reflection
- Change
  - Proactive

Knowledge

- Describe own role, responsibilities, values, and scope of practice effectively to clients/patients/families and other professionals.
- Describe IP theory with respect to the science and theories behind teamwork.
- Describe the context and culture of the IP environment that facilitates or inhibits collaboration, and its constraints.
- Identify instances where IP care will improve client/patient/family outcomes.

Communication

- Listening
- Giving and receiving feedback
- Sharing information effectively
- Common language
- Dealing with conflict

Knowledge

- Recognize and understand how one's own uniqueness, including power and hierarchy within the IP team, may contribute to effective communication and/or IP tension.
- Recognize and understand how the uniqueness of other team members, including power and hierarchy within the IP team, may contribute to effective communication and/or IP tension.

Values and Ethics

- Relational-centred
- Diversity sensitive
- Interdependence
- Creativity/innovation

Knowledge

- Describe IP team dynamics as they relate to individual team members' values and the impact on team functioning in ethical dilemmas.
- Describe the nature of IP ethical reasoning and justification.

Skill / Behaviour

- Identify IP ethical issues within a team context.
- Utilize the basic skills of reasoning and justification as it relates to identified ethical issues within an IP team.

Attitude

- Reflect on own values, personal and professional, and respect those of other IP team members/clients/families.
- Clarify values including accountability, respect, confidentiality, trust, integrity, honesty and ethical behaviour, equity as it relates to IP team functioning to maximize quality, safe patient care.

REFLECTION, LEARNING, AND

LEARNING

AND CORE COMPETENCIES—*Health Professional Programs, University of Toronto*

IMMERSION: DEVELOPMENT

COMPETENCE: ENTRY-TO-PRACTICE

Skill / Behaviour

- Accurately describe the roles, responsibilities, and scopes of practice of other professions.
- Contribute to:
  - Involving other professions in client/patient/family care appropriate to their roles and responsibilities.
  - Effective decision making in IP teamwork utilizing judgment and critical thinking.
  - Team effectiveness through reflection on IP team function.
  - Establishment and maintenance of effective IP working relationships/partnerships.

Skill / Behaviour

- Work collaboratively with others, as appropriate, to assess, plan, provide care/intervention, and make decisions to optimize client/patient/family health outcomes and improve quality of care.
- Demonstrate leadership in advancing effective IP team function through a variety of strategies including, but not limited to:
  - Reflection.
  - Promotion of effective decision making.
  - Identification of factors that contribute to or hinder team collaboration, including power and hierarchy.
  - Flexibility and adaptability.
  - Able to assume diverse roles in their IP group and support others in their roles.
  - Establish and maintain effective IP working relationship partnerships with clients/patients/ families and other team members, teams, and/or organizations to support achievement of common goals.

Attitude

- Based on client/patient/family needs, consider that preferred practice is IP collaboration and willingly collaborate.

Skill / Behaviour

- Contribute to effective IP communication, including:
  - Giving and receiving feedback
  - Addressing conflict or difference of opinions.
  - Self-reflecting.

Attitude

- Awareness of, and openness to utilize and develop, effective IP communication skills.

Skill / Behaviour

- Communicate effectively, including giving and receiving feedback.
- Advance IP group functioning through effectively addressing IP conflict.
- Perform as an effective IP team member by:
  - Sharing information.
  - Listening attentively.
  - Using understandable communications.
  - Providing feedback to others.
  - Responding to feedback from others.

Attitude

- Develop awareness of and contribute to continual improvement of IP team dynamics and group processes through effective IP communication.

Knowledge

- Describe frameworks for ethical decision making within an IP team.

Skill / Behaviour

- Guided by an ethics framework, contribute to IP ethical reasoning and decision making.

Attitude

- Advance values including accountability, respect, confidentiality, trust, integrity, honesty, and ethical behaviour, equity as it relates to IP team functioning to maximize quality, safe patient care.

Skill / Behaviour

- Perform effectively to develop shared team values.
- Practice ethically in an IP environment.
- Able to use a framework for ethical decision making to guide ethical reasoning within an IP team.

Attitude

- Accept, through respect and value, others and their contributions in relational-centred care.

SUMMATIVE ASSESSMENT

INTERPROFESSIONAL PARTNERSHIP AND COLLABORATIVE PRACTICE FOR OPTIMIZATION OF CLIENT/PATIENT HEALTH OUTCOMES

FORMATIVE ASSESSMENT

CONTINUUM ⟶

Figure 7—Framework for the Development of Interprofessional Education Values
© University of Toronto, Centre for Interprofessional Education

"At the end of the day, U of T is already a very academically challenging institution. As students in health care professional programs, we are spending a great deal of time engaging with our academic material, as well as our clinical placements. While IPE is certainly a valuable addition to our curriculum, we want to ensure that if health care students are required to participate in additional, mandatory education sessions, that such sessions are structured and delivered in a way which is beneficial to us from a student perspective."

– Elisa Simpson, nursing student
  and co-president of IPHSA

Because reflection is such a critical element of professional development as a student and practitioner, learners from several of the programs, including nursing, occupational science and occupational therapy, and speech-language pathology, currently complete guided reflective assignments based on IPE learning activities; these reflections are integrated into coursework and are added to a student's final portfolio. A more comprehensive assessment strategy focusing on knowledge of content and process, demonstration of competencies in a simulated environment, and action in a clinical environment is currently being developed.

In 2009, the University of Toronto's new Centre for IPE transitioned the foundational and innovative work in IPE to a requisite interprofessional curriculum for ten of its eleven health science programs (dentistry, medical radiation sciences, medicine, nursing, occupational therapy, pharmacy, physical therapy, physician assistant, social work, and speech-language pathology. Kinesiology will come online 2014–15). The formal U of T IPE curriculum is competency-based, longitudinal, and consists of four core learning activities—(1) Teamwork: Your Future in Interprofessional Health Care; (2) Case-Based Session (either Pain or Palliative Care); (3) Conflict in Interprofessional Life; and (4) IPE Component in a Clinical Placement—and a specified number of elective IPE learning opportunities. Each year a new cohort of 1,400 incoming first-year students arrive at the university and begin their participation in the IPE curriculum.

Arriving at consensus across health science programs to create a single curriculum on paper is an achievement in and of itself. But like all initiatives, the real test is in the implementation. There are challenges inherent in bringing together eleven health science programs to include IPE components into curricula that can be quite distinct and already packed with content. The curriculum framework creates the tables at which these issues can be addressed, and the collective vision

can be influenced by the priorities of each program. The IFCC and the multiple teams working with each of the curriculum offerings are negotiating and streamlining points that enable an ongoing and evolving discussion about IPE.

Another challenge exists in ensuring each student receives a similar IPE experience. As one would expect when bringing into alignment two-, three-, and four-year programs at the undergraduate and graduate levels, the structure of the curriculum does vary slightly program to program, but the four core learning activities are always present. Along with these core learning activities, individual health sciences programs currently determine how many elective learning activities students in their faculty/department will complete. Efforts to promote consistency among all eleven of the health science programs are guided by the Interfaculty Curriculum Committee.

YEAR 1 INTRODUCTORY SESSION—TEAMWORK: YOUR FUTURE IN INTERPROFESSIONAL HEALTH CARE

The Year 1 introductory session on teamwork has a special feel to it. Convocation Hall at U of T seats over 1,200 people. It is an iconic building for the university, which adds to the significance of this event for the freshman class. It will be where they convocate in two, three, or four years. In many ways, this represents the start and end of their journey as a health sciences student. A lighthearted mood pervades the event. Students fill the dark stadium in designated seating, placed away from their classmates in teams that represent the multiple professional programs represented. When the session begins, the facilitator (in 2012 it was Dr. Stephanie Nixon, a lively physical therapy professor) with a head mike and lots of attitude, calls out for all the different individual programs, and the students cheer from across the interprofessional clusters, identifying themselves as each program is named. It feels more like a sporting than academic event. Everyone is having fun and there to learn about their own new profession and those it intersects with.

With a large student cohort and multiple health professional programs to coordinate, the Year 1 session team has determined the single

"It's easier not to do something than it is to do something. Deans and Chairs need to take responsibility for IPE, lead it, and not be cynical or dismissive about it being another fad. To be in a leadership role and say you're going to keep the status quo is an abdication of your responsibilities."

– Sioban Nelson, Nursing at U of T

date, single venue, and two-hour format is the most effective. The physical presence of everyone in the same lecture hall, hearing the same messages from IPE and health care leaders, communicates two powerful messages: first, that health care serves patients and their needs, and second, that care providers are team members.

One technique that has proven successful in reinforcing these messages is to purposely organize preassigned seating to enable students to engage with an interprofessional (six-member) group in proximity to their seats. Approximately one hundred facilitators, drawn from a wide range of practices and professions, are each assigned two groups. They serve to clarify issues, validate roles, and stimulate engagement among the learners. Facilitator feedback confirms the presence of students' positive energy and realization of the importance the university places on teamwork. The agenda begins with brief remarks from two or three senior professional and/or practice leaders. Organizers emphasize that speakers need to be enthusiastic supporters of IPE, painting the picture of why IPE is important in the context of providing the best health care possible. This is followed by a patient sharing her personal story of an experience with the health care system. The patient voice acts as a powerful anchor and represents the essence of why students choose to go into health care in the first place: to make a difference for patients and families. Guerrilla theatre–style skits depicting functional and dysfunctional IP teams are then performed by faculty members (in collaboration with actors from the Standardized Patient Program) to allow students to see and hear words used by future colleagues; critical discussion then ensues in a safe environment.

Educators have learned they need to be acutely sensitive to each line of the script included in the simulations because new learners are attending closely to their specific role and how it is portrayed. The organizers have realized a great deal of thought needs to go into the skits to ensure they neither idealize nor stereotype professional roles in practice. This is a challenge in that the purpose of the skits is to highlight some of the dysfunctional communication that students will most certainly

"I was unsure about whether or not this experience was going to be worth all of the scheduling challenges and time commitments, but as soon as I met my mentor and started to hear her story, I was hooked."

– Student feedback, Health Mentor Program

encounter at some stage as learners in the practice setting. Maureen Barry, senior lecturer in the Faculty of Nursing, recalls the distress experienced by one enthusiastic nursing faculty member when some years ago students complained to the dean that the nursing faculty member's portrayal of nursing in a skit made them reconsider their decision to study nursing. This type of feedback is brought into the formal debrief of faculty organizers to ensure that changes to the script are considered, as well as enhancements made to facilitator orientation related to how they handle stereotypes that are surfaced during the session. Part of the process has been for facilitators to develop an acute awareness of how students, particularly new students, see their respective professions. The scripts are now developed with these sensitivities in mind—showing the challenges without threatening the students' early professional identities. Care is taken to depict the specific strengths each team member brings to understanding the case study without resorting to narrow stereotypes where doctors care only about the diagnosis, pharmacists only about medication, and nurses only about psychosocial care. It's a delicate balance, and one that has become easier with experience, building each year on student feedback.

Small group discussions are interspersed with all of the above elements, and assigned facilitators are available for guidance. Organizers have found over the years that a mix of short on-stage presentations interspersed with small group discussion has been most effective to generate engagement with the learners. Concluding remarks provided by student IPE leaders highlight future IPE sessions in the curriculum.

Through its evolution over the past number of years, planners of this introductory session have faced several challenges. The most significant has been to attain commitment from all professions to include the session as a required part of the curriculum and, related to this, to find a common time and convenient location. Persistence of IPE "champions" within each profession has been critically important in gaining this

> "Many times students have shared with me how much my story changed the way they would relate to their clients, and redefined their perceived limits of stroke recovery to be open-minded and hopeful – that to me is worth gold because I know more stroke survivors out there will be encouraged to have hope and better care."
>
> – Health Mentor

"Our dental curriculum is packed. Students are here from 8am to 5pm, and we try to give them a lunch break. It's hard to find room for interprofessional learning, but it's also absolutely essential."

– Daniel Haas, the dean of Dentistry at U of T

commitment and maintaining everyone's engagement.

Andrea Cameron, senior lecturer in pharmacy, believes the success of the session emanates from students' being together at this formative moment of their learning, meeting new colleagues who share common hopes and goals. Every year she sees that the introductory session allows learners to "begin their interprofessional journey with a new appreciation for one another."

THE TIMETABLE SQUEEZE: RETOOLING OTHER COURSES

After the introductory learning activity, learners engage in one of two case-based sessions in order to meet the core requirements of the IPE curriculum, either Pain or Palliative Care. The Pain Curriculum, governed by the Centre for IPE but developed and delivered by the Centre for the Study of Pain at U of T, is another example, along with the introductory learning activity, of a pre-existing curriculum activity with committed core faculty that was integrated into the IPE curriculum when it was rolled out.

In 2002, the Centre for the Study of Pain implemented the first iteration of the Pain Curriculum that has both uniprofessional and interprofessional elements. At that time, there was much resistance to the idea of IPE from some of the health sciences. Questions were raised concerning its value to uniprofessional programs and its fit with the content. There was also a great deal of skepticism on the impact of interprofessional curricula on uniprofessional educational outcomes. Professor Emeritus Judy Watt-Watson, Faculty of Nursing, recalls how much work was involved in overcoming this resistance. Advocates needed to build an interfaculty team and then visit the curriculum committees of each of the health sciences for input. This process allowed faculty across the health sciences to engage with the idea of interprofessional curriculum. When they developed the Pain Curriculum, organizers understood that the health sciences were siloed from one another, and students were arriving with preconceived assumptions and stereotypes of other health professions. Early on, the Pain Curriculum offered a chance to develop a new approach to education by introducing pioneering concepts in IPE. First, students were oriented to the fact that this was a different kind of curriculum. After

this, student assessments were conducted to determine biases and understandings toward other health science professions and IPE in general. Once the curriculum began, students were divided into groups of approximately thirty to thirty-six students, then further broken down into teams of ten to twelve, each with two to three co-facilitators—some with interprofessional facilitation experience and some with pain-related expertise. These facilitators are academic and status-appointed clinical faculty sourced from all over the Greater Toronto Area, ensuring a breadth of expertise and training by representatives from the Centre for IPE and Centre for the Study of Pain.

Case-based learning and conflict resolution were identified as priorities in approach and content, along with working in interprofessional teams on clinically focused issues. The development of the Pain Curriculum was also seen as an opportunity to address some of the misconceptions surrounding IPE. Over the three-and-a-half-day Pain Curriculum, students attend plenary sessions on pain that include experiences of patients, as well as concurrent breakout sessions. An important component is the facilitated interprofessional group work. This starts with a case-based study on acute pain, which then moves to persistent pain. Teams of students focus on developing a pain assessment and management plan, and must develop this plan together. This activity is massive, with approximately thirty groups of thirty students, each with three facilitators. At the end of the curriculum, students are assessed again for their biases and understandings in self-reflective exercises.

Organizers are clear that the Pain Curriculum is not solely focused on IPE; rather, it is an example of a blended uniprofessional and interprofessional curriculum focused on the content of pain that incorporates IPE. The focus is on pain management but within an interprofessional context that is necessary to provide effective care. The interprofessional components include group work centred around cases and the development of integrated care plans, and students earn recognition for these under the IPE curriculum framework. In this way, the Pain Curriculum serves as an exemplar of how IPE can be integrated into uniprofessional programming.

For some faculty, there is an important philosophical difference between the way the Pain Curriculum

"You don't have your professional identity yet. That's something that's hard about IPE – we're still developing our professional identities but we're also asked to understand everyone else's professional identities."

– Nikki Fischer, medical student at U of T

organizers think about IPE and the way the IPE curriculum is structured overall. For the Pain group, the focus is clinical, and teamwork and communication are part of solving the practice problem. An interprofessional approach is required to solve these complex issues, and students hear from patient facilitators about the effect of siloed and limited approaches to the management of their chronic pain. As myths and false beliefs are explicitly targeted by the curriculum, there is a focus on attitude and self-awareness—important components in interprofessional practice. In the end, the focus of the Pain Curriculum is both on the "what" of the learning (pain-related content) and the "how" of the learning (interprofessional learning). Preparation of the facilitators therefore focuses not only on pain content but critically on developing interprofessional facilitation expertise as well.

Although the Pain Curriculum is a popular choice for students in many of the health sciences programs to meet the core requirements of the IPE curriculum, integrating existing curriculum into the IPE curriculum was not without challenges. With the implementation of a requisite IPE curriculum in 2009 (seven years after the Pain Curriculum had already been in place), two groups of leaders with some overlapping faculty needed to come together to understand and plan for the intricacies of integrating Pain into the IPE curriculum. The structures that govern these two areas have since been clarified and aligned, highlighting the great similarities in approaches and the opportunity to work together to bring strengths of each into respective programming.

The Pain Curriculum takes an indirect approach to IPE teaching, incorporating issues of interprofessional team communication and collaboration via case studies, as opposed to curriculum content that directly addresses team functioning. This tension between a course promoting teamwork and interpersonal values versus clinical content and skill building is a familiar one for all health professional educators. Students (and some faculty) tend to be resistant to "soft" content or what they see as navel-gazing. Some of this debate is historical. Starting a conversation about how professions work together—if they are civil and respectful of each other's knowledge, if they know enough about each other and have the skills to ask for input and foster collaborative practice—can

> "We have to get past the fear that we will get into a scheduling conflict. You don't need a classroom the size of a hockey arena to put all the students in so you can teach them together."
>
> – Sarita Verma, the deputy dean of Medicine at U of T

be uncomfortable for students and faculty. Depending on how much the student is attached to a certain view of their own profession and assumptions about others, discussion can raise hackles and reinforce stereotypes rather than address and challenge them. For this reason, strong facilitation skills are required and champions within each faculty are critical to prevent offense and disengagement that will lead to a drift back into silos.

One school of thought, personified in the Pain Curriculum, is that the focus of curriculum is on the patient not the provider. By this means, a more tactical approach to advancing collaboration is to come somewhat obliquely at the issue of team performance. This perspective contends that discussions concerning team communication and effective team relations are more readily accepted by learners through the vehicle of case examples and strong facilitation than through the more direct or didactic approach.

In practice, both approaches (content on collaboration generically and common content such as pain and palliative care) are critical. For example, a core competency related to navigating tension within health care teams led to the development of the third core requirement within the IPE curriculum: Conflict in Interprofessional Life. Students view a lecture online, complete a self-assessment to determine their preferred method of conflict resolution, and gather face-to-face to meet in interprofessional groups for the experiential component of the learning activity. To warm up to their student teams, they review material and participate in an icebreaker. Then they view, discuss, and interact with a conflict scenario. Facilitators encourage an understanding of roles and guide the practice of new strategies.

> "The minute you say you're going to have a session on collaboration, you lose learners. Face it: A lot of learners are overwhelmed by the volume of factual information they need to absorb, so that's where they'll put their money."
>
> – Salvatore Spadafora, vice-dean of Postgraduate Medical Education at U of T

FITTING MORE INTO THE CURRICULUM

The idea that everything you add to the curriculum must be balanced by the removal of content creates intense conflict among faculty members who are committed to seeing their areas of priority given due prominence in curricula. For instance, if I am a primary care or public health professional, I am automatically concerned by any increase in course time devoted to acute inpatient care. However well-justified and

NUMBER OF ELECTIVES WITHIN THE IPE CURRICULUM

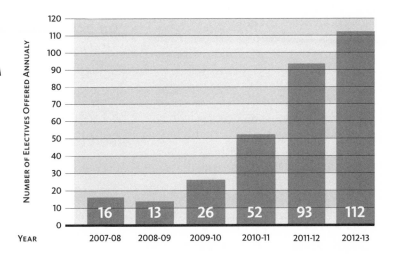

AVAILABLE SPACES ACROSS IPE ELECTIVES

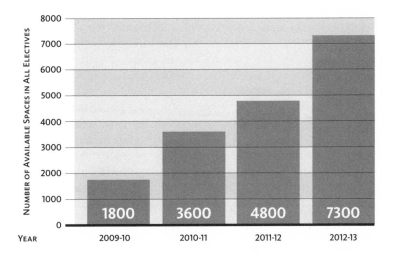

Figure 8—Growth and Expansion in Electives

well-meaning this political dimension of curriculum planning is, for the IPE innovators it meant space had to be found without dislodging any other content. This complicated diplomatic negotiation of space in the curriculum revolved around identifying some fundamental core activities and then creating IPE electives that could be offered in a wide range of times, formats, and settings. This variety of offerings provided the opportunity for IPE options to be responsive to student needs. By this approach, student interests (e.g., in topics such as dying and death, medication reconciliation, and difficult conversations) can be followed, and at the same time faculty enthusiasm leveraged, allowing for an expansion of content to students in key areas. If a number of faculty wanted to high-

light an area of practice from an interprofessional perspective, it is a simple process to have this idea incorporated into the formal IPE curriculum, whether it be a short program (a couple of hours) or an extended one (multiple sessions). In this way the issue of curriculum "space" was not only managed, but leveraged to increase content in popular areas.

Many faculty and clinicians are educated to be facilitators and contribute to the development of new and innovative learning activities. Students have the opportunity to participate in approximately 120 IPE elective learning activities in many areas (e.g., mental health, quality and safety, risk management, chronic health challenges, and ethics), and the number grows each year. Coordination of IPE activities is massive; with an intake of approximately 1,400 students each year, there can be a total of 3,700 students completing IPE curriculum requirements at any given time.

In this section, we present a series of case studies to demonstrate timetabling for IPE, the range of electives, and a solution to finding curriculum space for IPE.

The Ultimate Challenge: Finding Space for IPE

What defeats all but the most determined and strategic implementers of IPE is the "space" question. Space refers to time in the curriculum, room within the overloaded course content, and a physical space for learners to come together—sometimes in large numbers.

As health care evolves, new knowledge emerges that can transform the way we understand phenomena. This new evidence needs to be constantly brought into the curriculum and outdated ideas revised and filtered out. In addition to this endless refresh of content to reflect the latest thinking, health professional curricula are subject to intense pressure from government, interest groups, regulators, and multiple other stakeholders. Advocacy groups dissatisfied with the current state of care in everything from end-of-life care to patient safety constantly lobby for mandated content to be incorporated into the curricula of health professionals and for regulators or accreditation agencies to ensure that information on these topics is part of health professional education. The result has been twofold. First, all health professional curricula are bursting at the seams with mandated hours on multiple topics. Second, educators have developed antibodies to the endless call for more content on X or Y topics. Overcoming these antibodies and the to-be-expected cynicism among some faculty that IPE is simply a trendy new fad are the first two barriers to getting faculty to work together to find the space for an integrated interprofessional curriculum.

In addition to the issue of faculty guarding curriculum time, students need to understand that IPE is worth prioritizing. Health professional students are busy people. They have packed schedules of classes at the university and typically

spend many days of the week off campus in practice settings. In recent years there has been a steady growth in simulation components for nursing, pharmacy, social work, dentistry, medical, and rehabilitation science students. Simply getting through the curriculum while juggling the rest of their lives is quite an achievement. University of Toronto students are typically high-achieving individuals whose health professional program represents their second or third degree. They have family responsibilities, engage in volunteer activities, and often pursue hobbies. Finding time for anything more in their school lives is enormously difficult, and—as pragmatic, intelligent, and forthright individuals—they have no intention of wasting their time on activities that are not meaningful. They arrive at the university with intentions and expectations to participate in curricula that builds their capacities as members of health care teams.

At U of T, the approach was to first think carefully about how much common curriculum time could be achieved and then, working hard with the support of the deans and program directors, to create space in the curriculum for IPE. This meant that some curricular activities involved all of the health sciences (e.g., Year 1 session), while others were targeted to smaller numbers of students where it may be most relevant for specific professional programs to work together to create integrated curricular time and content (e.g., a medication reconciliation elective across

medicine, nursing, and pharmacy).

Symbolically, the early focus on IPE in the curriculum communicates to learners that interprofessional activities are part of being a U of T health sciences student; and that everyone should think of him- or herself as a member of the health team right from the start. The IFCC team was committed to the idea of an introductory core learning activity (Teamwork: Your Future in Interprofessional Health Care) to solidify the notion that this group of 1,400 first-year students is a cohort. The assumption underlying the Year 1 session on teamwork is that it is necessary to get to the students early in their program to make them aware that they are part of a broader health care team and that they need to learn about team-based practice. More subtly, the idea is communicated that by learning about the team, one also understands one's own practice and builds one's dual identity as a member of a given profession and as a team member. This exercise aims to foster a patient-centric, as opposed to a siloed, provider-centric, professional identity.

As of 2013, Teamwork: Your Future in Interprofessional Health Care had been running at the University of Toronto for twelve years. For each of those years, the challenge has been the same: find the space, get everyone involved, and keep all the faculty and students engaged. Faculty engagement is particularly crucial because students take their cues from fac-

ulty. If their professional role models see IPE as meaningful to their uniprofessional program, the students will be keen to participate. Over the years the session has been held in all kinds of venues, and, as the enrolments for health sciences grew over the time, the scale of the learning activity became a major challenge. The event has finally achieved pole position, taking place in Convocation Hall each year.

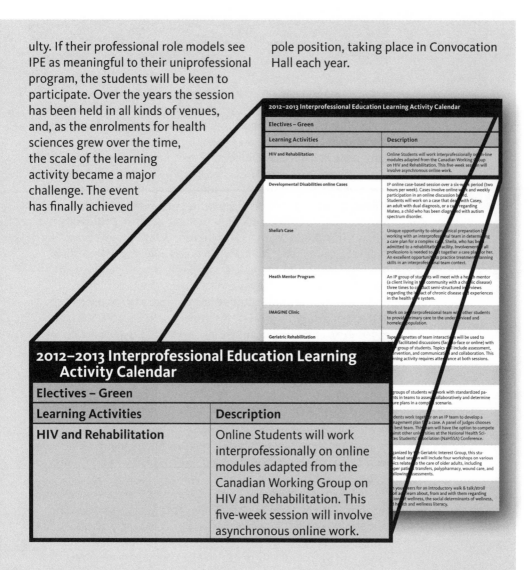

2012–2013 Interprofessional Education Learning Activity Calendar

Electives – Green	
Learning Activities	**Description**
HIV and Rehabilitation	Online Students will work interprofessionally on-line modules adapted from the Canadian Working Group on HIV and Rehabilitation. This five-week session will involve asynchronous online work.
Developmental Disabilities online Cases	IP online case-based session over a six-week period (two hours per week). Cases involve online work and weekly participation in an online discussion board. Students will work on a case that deals with Casey, an adult with dual diagnosis, or a case regarding Mateo, a child who has been diagnosed with autism spectrum disorder.
Shelia's Case	Unique opportunity to obtain clinical preparation by working with an interprofessional team in determining a care plan for a complex case, Sheila, who has been admitted to a rehabilitation facility. Involvement of all professions is needed to put together a care plan for her. An excellent opportunity to practice treatment planning skills in an interprofessional team context.
Heath Mentor Program	An IP group of students will meet with a health mentor (a client living in the community with a chronic disease) three times to conduct semi-structured interviews regarding the impact of chronic disease and experiences in the health care system.
IMAGINE Clinic	Work on an interprofessional team with other students to provide primary care to the underserviced and homeless population.
Geriatric Rehabilitation	Taped vignettes of team interactions will be used to facilitated discussions (face-to-face or online) with a group of students. Topics will include assessment, intervention, and communication and collaboration. This learning activity requires attendance at both sessions.
	groups of students will work with standardized patients in teams to assess collaboratively and determine care plans in a complex scenario.
	students work together on an IP team to develop a management plan for a case. A panel of judges chooses the best team. This team will have the option to compete against other universities at the National Health Sciences Students' Association (NaHSSA) Conference.
	organized by the Geriatric Interest Group, this student-lead session will include four workshops on various topics related to the care of older adults, including proper patient transfers, polypharmacy, wound care, and allowing assessments.
	with your peers for an introductory walk & talk/stroll and learn about, from and with them regarding notion of wellness, the social determinants of wellness, health and wellness literacy.

Figure 9—
Sample Elective

CASE STUDY 1
Dying and Death

A PERSON WHO IS DYING MAY LIVE FOR SOME TIME WITH A PALLIATIVE prognosis. In this protracted period of time, one's social, emotional, occupational, and fiscal resources diminish. Each person's death has a ripple effect across many people. With life extension, familial caregiving demands endurance and resiliency, even with health care support, and, over time, impacts everyone's well-being. People may begin to wish for death as the quality of their life diminishes. With team support and guidance, the dying person can be the most powerful agent to help anticipate adaptations and orchestrate the family's life after a death has taken place. While there is no curing (from the Latin curare, to fix) when one is palliative, there can be healing (from Anglo-Saxon haelan, making more whole) if death is attended to by an interprofessional team.

The Dying and Death elective learning activity has deep roots in the U of T's interprofessional community. It began in the late 1990s as an initiative led largely by the University Chaplaincy group. As a collaborative endeavor across the faiths, with committed representation from health sciences programs, patients, and volunteers, it offers the opportunity for students to learn about and prepare for one of the big challenges of a health professional's role—knowing what to say to and how to manage families and patients during the dying process and at the time of death.

Because the subject matter is so powerful, "students all fear that they will do or say the 'wrong thing'," says Maureen Barry, senior lecturer at the Faculty of Nursing and long-time lead for nursing in this IPE elective. The session allows them to ask candid questions of the different chaplains and each other as to what would be appropriate in this or that instance and to learn, perhaps their first actual exposure, about the different religious and spiritual responses to dying and death from Toronto's diverse community members. The elective clearly meets a major need for students, so much so that the Centre for IPE has had to increase the opportunities for students to attend this session based on waiting lists, making it one of a handful of electives offered twice per academic year, accommodating 250 learners in all.

A foundational principle of the elective is care for the caregiver. In a room with round tables, each accommodating six or seven learners from across a range of health care professions and two facilitators, seats are preassigned to replicate diverse IP teams. The learners are greeted, seated, and offered a meal, fostering learning and self-care. The meal itself has been a key element of the event with the entire team considering taking food together as a group highly symbolic of the commitment to share and work together

and the ability to find common ground. In the early days there were challenges in bringing the different faiths together; Jody Macdonald, senior lecturer in nursing and lead in the early 2000s, recalls heated debates over the issue of saying grace. (In the end, no grace was said.) At the time, much was learned by the team about sensitive issues of religious and spiritual practice and about their impact on the ability to work together and effectively communicate in everyday contexts, much less at extraordinary times such as those surrounding death.

As with all the IPE learning activities, the problems of space and resources continue to challenge. Over the years, the Dying and Death elective was run in all kinds of spaces, and the meal supported from various sources. In 2012 it was held in the basement of St. Patrick's Parish, and the meal provided (and home cooked) by the hospice volunteers.

Dinner is typically followed by three speakers, each representing their own disciplinary approach to the topic. Although they have seldom worked together, it becomes evident that the speakers share the interprofessionalism integral to collaborative, patient- and family-centered practice around dying and death. For example, the social work representative may speak about the need for family education and counseling, which can be undertaken only after medicine, nursing, and physical therapy achieve the symptom relief that enables the patient and family to fully use social work interventions.

All teams work on the same case, with a recorder for each team. The room becomes a cacophony of voices and high energy. After forty-five minutes, each table presents their findings, invariably raising the same issues. The last tables are challenged to refine rather than replicate the care plan. One guest speaker integrates the presentations into a complex care plan, demonstrating scaffolding of care.

For Michele Chaban, social work adjunct professor: "It's a really intense and powerful few hours. The students, facilitators, and faculty are all fully engaged. We always conclude with a mindfulness exercise, centering participants in gratitude for a room of healers in end-of-life care. The students leave with a vision and experience of how interprofessionalism makes a profound difference to care of the dying person and their family. It's a very special experience."

CASE STUDY 2
Health Mentor Program

THE PATIENT/CLIENT IS THE MOST IMPORTANT MEMBER OF THE interprofessional team, and in this elective, health science students have the privilege of being mentored by an individual who

has had multiple encounters with the health care system. As the students meet with an individual who has a chronic health challenge, identified as a mentor, they develop an understanding of how a disease or condition can affect daily life. They expand their knowledge of the roles that various health professionals have in a patient's care. And most critically, they learn the extent to which a health care provider's words and actions can affect a patient.

Inspired by a health mentor program at Thomas Jefferson University in Philadelphia, Sylvia Langlois, current Faculty Lead, Curriculum at the Centre for IPE, adapted Jefferson's two-year IPE model to the needs of an elective for first-year health science students. Langlois has been involved in IPE at U of T from its earliest days, and she has been the innovator behind many of the early IPE electives. Her first challenge: Find community members with a chronic health condition who would be willing to mentor health science students. "Initially, recruiting was hard," recalls Langlois, who is also an assistant professor in U of T's Department of Occupational Science and Occupational Therapy. "Finding potential health mentors took most of the summer." By approaching individuals already involved in patient/client advocacy, she eventually found twenty-five volunteers, with conditions ranging from multiple sclerosis, rheumatoid arthritis, and post-stroke or traumatic brain injury to those who are HIV positive or have aphasia and use assistive technology to communicate. Others have multiple chronic conditions. The parents of a child with disabilities also stepped forward and volunteered. While the mentors are affected by different diagnoses, throughout the elective they share a common goal: to improve patient/client care by promoting a collaborative response to chronic health challenges.

The elective has grown in popularity. Now in its fifth year, it draws 150 health science students annually and needs more than thirty mentors. "Most of the volunteers come back year after year," says Langlois. "Occasionally, though, the disease exacerbates and it's just too difficult for them." Some mentors find it personally rewarding and beneficial. As one mentor put it, "I always leave these sessions feeling as if a weight has been taken off my shoulders."

Every year, Langlois starts off the program by providing the mentors with an orientation session at the university. She goes over the program's goals and encourages them to share their first hand experiences with the health care system. "The program allows individ-

"Meeting with these bright minds as they study their chosen career path is exciting. I have found that exploring their mindsets and having an open two-way discussion has given me insights into how I have not let my illness define me."

– Health mentor

uals to tell their story in a constructive way. I don't bring into the program any people who have an axe to grind," she says.

Langlois then assigns an interprofessional group of four or five health science students to each mentor. The students and mentor arrange to meet either on a weekday evening or Saturday morning. Typically, they meet in the university's health sciences building. The Centre for IPE covers the mentors' transportation costs; otherwise, some individuals may be unable to volunteer.

The students and mentor get together three times. The students lead the interview, which is guided by a semistructured interview format. "This ensures they consider the breadth of the issues involved," says Langlois. "For example, safety is typically seen as being related to medication errors and falls, but there are broader issues involving psychosocial issues and communication." The interviews explore the impact of chronic illness in the context of the person's life and explore the idea of a collaborative assessment. Two key foci are ethical/professionalism and patient/client safety issues.

One health mentor describes how the interviews evolve. "At each of the sittings the questions become more complex, more involved and philosophical. I have enjoyed learning of their career paths and questioned what has led them to this point." After completing each interview, the students participate in a facilitated interprofessional online discussion or face-to-face discussion group. At the end of the elective, they write a reflection paper. Their reflections reveal myriad insights into what it feels like to be on the receiving end of health care. Some students vow never to dismiss a patient/client's feelings. Others come to recognize the importance of interprofessional communication and teamwork with medications; one student wrote, "A client's psychological and physical well-being, as well as their life, depends on it."

While students cite difficulties in arranging times to meet with their mentor, the elective consistently scores excellent feedback.

CASE STUDY 3
Orientation to IPE: The IPHSA Elective

THE INTERPROFESSIONAL HEALTHCARE STUDENTS' ASSOCIATION (IPHSA) hosts its own IPE elective, an orientation to interprofessional education. This is a completely IPHSA-run event, which changes from year to year to reflect changes in the student representation on IPHSA and students' individual stamp on the session. That stamp will often reflect the professional interests of the student leaders.

In 2012 student leaders designed the session so that the various representatives on IPHSA introduced their profession to the class. Students then were given a case study, which was first discussed through a uniprofessional lens. Nurses who were in attendance, for example, met with their lead facilitator and discussed how they would approach this case from a nursing perspective. Next, the case was discussed within an interprofessional group, with the various professions explaining how they would approach the patient case. Elisa Simpson, former co-president of IPHSA, describes it as a "really fantastic, entirely student-run event that is both fun and educational for all involved. Even as student facilitators, we have a lot of fun designing and delivering the content! It is traditionally very well attended, and this year wasn't any different."

And it continues to evolve. Medicine student and IPHSA Co-President Kaspar Ng describes how the student leaders aim to be very responsive to student feedback. In 2012, they received feedback that students didn't know a lot about chiropractic and naturopathic medicine. In response, IPHSA and the student council at the Canadian College of Naturopathic Medicine organized a week where students can sign up and shadow a naturopathic doctor or student either in the classroom or in one of their clinics to get a better immersion and understanding of what they do. Their plans don't stop there, either. Ng adds, "We are looking to set this up so students can shadow professionals in other faculties as well."

> CASE STUDY 4
> *IPE Online*

DEVELOPING ONLINE IPE OPPORTUNITIES CAN MITIGATE THE LOGIS-tical challenges that arise when attempting to organize an activity for students from different departments and faculties. But when a student sits at a computer to learn, does it provide the same level of engagement and depth of understanding as face-to-face learning? To help build our understanding of these issues and inform future interprofessional learning activities, U of T's "Developing Team-Based Collaboration and Communication Competency in Geriatrics" team developed an elective and research study that compared the learning differences in synchronous online and face-to-face interactions. The study also charted how to develop blended (i.e., combined face-to-face and online) learning opportunities and examined student preferences.

The elective includes four sets of video scenarios. Each set contains two videos: In one video the interprofessional team

collaborates in a less-than-effective manner, and in the other they communicate and collaborate better. By comparing the two interactions, the students not only further their interprofessional competencies but also grow to understand the need for teamwork when caring for seniors. "Interprofessional care is crucial with the elderly because seniors can have complex needs, including chronic, acute, as well as psychosocial issues," says Langlois, the study's lead investigator.

For the study, the students were divided into two groups. In one group, the students first discussed two sets of videos in a classroom and then the remaining videos together online. In the other group, the students first discussed the same two sets of videos online and then watched the other videos in a classroom. Student feedback was a mix of positive and negative responses, reflecting different learner styles and preferences. The difference in the level of engagement with the content and with fellow learners was statistically significant when students began with the online activity first. When they started with the face-to-face component, they had a significant drop in engagement with content and peers when they moved to online. This suggests it may be better to start with an online component and move to a face-to-face component. Future plans for online learning will be building on this student feedback.

In a second online learning module, this time coming out of the Centre for Addiction and Mental Health (CAMH), the team discovered that creating an online learning module can be surprisingly time-consuming. The Perspectives™ interprofessional team rushed to meet an eighteen-month deadline in which they were to create two online modules, embed them in a learning management system, and pilot each module once. "There's the whole technical aspect on top of the content. It was a tough slog," notes Susan Morris, a social worker and clinical director of the Dual Diagnosis Service at CAMH.

Through the Perspectives™ program, three health care organizations partner to engage health science students in how they can make a positive difference in the lives of individuals with developmental disabilities. "The training about this population is spotty at best," continues Morris, adding that Perspectives™ is open to health science students at U of T, two other local universities, and one college. "Student involvement is 'paid' for in kind," she explains. "For example, if one of the school's professors becomes a facilitator, her students can participate."

Interprofessional care is essential for individuals with developmental disabilities, says Morris. "Our clients have a high incidence of medical and psychiatric comorbidities, so each individual requires a team of health care providers. When care for this population is not provided interprofessionally, it causes

tremendous frustration for the families." To promote IPC, the module includes a video clip of a member of each health care profession involved in care. In one video, for instance, a dentist describes why he often needs to use a general anesthetic to conduct a checkup of a patient with a developmental disorder.

Morris contributed to the curriculum in the "Help Casey— Dual Diagnosis" online module. This elective begins with a face-to-face introductory seminar with the two facilitators and up to thirty students from a variety of health science programs. Unlike the "Competency in Geriatrics" study, the evaluation of Perspectives™ indicated that students prefer meeting with their facilitators and fellow students before starting the online component.

In the online modules, the students learn individually and contribute to online discussion groups facilitated by an expert in IPE and an expert in developmental disabilities. It takes students about ten hours to complete the six-week program. In the evaluation, 95 percent of the students said they would recommend the program to their peers.

> ### CASE STUDY 5
> ## *Medication Reconciliation*

MEDICATION RECONCILIATION IS A FORMAL PROCESS OF REVIEW of the total medications an individual is taking—prescribed and over the counter. It works best when it involves multiple members of the health care team. "It makes a lot of sense to teach medication reconciliation interprofessionally," points out Dr. Dante Morra, former associate director at the Centre for IPE. "Medication reconciliation is done across doctors, nurses, and pharmacists in the real world. No one participant has the natural power to do it alone. The learning activity provides the same content for everyone, and it's equally important to each participant; it's all the same learning."

Complex procedures that require a diversity of skills are those most suited to interprofessional learning, says Morra. "Simple or specific tasks don't need IPC. You don't need an interprofessional team to do a joint aspiration, for example. What I always say is that if you want to move a pencil across a table, you don't need a team. In fact, the team will get in the way."

The three-hour "Safe Prescribing: An Interprofessional Approach" learning activity brings together about 230 third-year medical students, 20 students training to be physician assistants, and 40 third- and fourth-year pharmacy students (all undergraduates), and it is currently being expanded to include (graduate) nurse practitioner students. The objectives of the ac-

tivity include identifying best practices in medication prescribing and dispensing; understanding your profession's role and responsibilities regarding medication practices; and identifying the role of interprofessional collaboration and communication in patient safety.

The activity begins with a large-group session in which medical patient safety models are reviewed, and students begin to identify the junctures at which a medication error could occur. Then the students break into small interprofessional groups to work through several cases that highlight common medication errors.

When the students return to the lecture hall, a senior pharmacist facilitates a discussion of the errors and introduces steps to avoid them. During the discussion, the students learn a couple of disturbing facts: More than one in six patients put on medications after seeing their family practitioner is given a prescription containing an error. Also, 1.5 million preventable adverse drug events occur every year in the United States.[2] And, more often than not, these events arise from a breakdown in interprofessional communication.

All the more reason to teach interprofessionally, says Morra, who is now the chief of medical staff at Trillium Health Partners in Toronto. He believes health science educators are on the verge of making IPE the norm. While today the curriculum is typically planned uniprofessionally and then IPE is added on, he predicts that one day the opposite will take place: IPE will become the planning principle, and uniprofessional activities will be added on.

CASE STUDY 6
Let's Not Play House

THE "LET'S NOT PLAY HOUSE" ELECTIVE GRABBED STUDENTS' attention from the get-go with its intriguing name, which references the popular television medical drama about Dr. House, who heads a diagnostic program for the most challenging cases wheeled through the doors of the fictitious Princeton–Plainsboro Teaching Hospital. Far from being an interprofessional team player, Dr. House consults only with other physicians and then only fleetingly. "Dr. House is uniprofessional," says Langlois. "No, he's worse than that. House pretty well listens only to himself."

The elective engaged the students by challenging them to solve a health care mystery. The evening started with sixty-five senior health science students assembling in a lecture hall and watching a short video about William, age fifty-nine, who had been admit-

ted to the hospital with respiratory failure, ataxia, confusion, flat affect, abdominal pain, and tremors. The students then broke into nine interprofessional groups; each group moved to a separate room along with two facilitators. The students' task: to assess William and develop an interprofessional plan for his care.

The students spent thirty minutes preparing for the assessment and then were able to invite William, portrayed as a standardized patient (by an actor), into the room. Each student could ask William—who walked in using a cane and dressed in a hospital gown—questions that arose from his or her professional lens. The students could also interview other actors who played William's two sons, his next-door neighbor, and a friend. As the student teams explored a variety of differential diagnoses, they could order specific tests and assessments—including blood work, magnetic resonance imaging (MRI), a detailed occupational therapy assessment, and dental records—and get instant results from one of their facilitators.

Langlois, an occupational therapist, created the case-based simulation with an interprofessional team that included faculty members from speech-language pathology, medical radiation sciences, physical therapy, nursing, pharmacy, dentistry, social work, and medicine. To engage the students, the team quickly realized they needed a case that was both complex and intriguing. Since they plan to repeat the learning activity, they're not willing to share what makes this case so compelling. The students won't share either. "We made the students sign a confidentiality agreement," says Langlois. "They're sworn to secrecy."

The simulation allows students to practice interviewing, assessment, critical thinking, and treatment planning in the context of an interprofessional team. "Every profession holds a key piece of information," explains Langlois. "The students can only solve the medical mystery by collaborating interprofessionally."

The drawback to the elective is that it's expensive, says Langlois (and for this reason has been only mounted once to date). To run the simulation for sixty-five students, the team hired ten actors to play standardized patients. (Each actor played William and other characters.) Impressed by the elective's innovative approach, the Standardized Patient Program at U of T awarded the project a grant to fund the actors. While the ability to interview actors portraying the patient, family members, and friends added to the critical thinking component of the learning activity, Langlois says the program may be adapted so that video clips replace the actors. "Authenticity is a particularly important element of Centre for IPE learning activities," she says. "Although the way the case was played out was not entirely authentic, the use of standardized patients provided a wonderful component."

ELECTIVES NOT ONLY REPRESENT A WIDE RANGE OF CONTENT
areas and formats, they also provide the opportunity for novel
approaches to learning about teams and team practice. A group
at the University Health Network (UHN), Mandy Lowe, and Patti
McGillicuddy in partnership with Karen Gold from Women's College Hospital, set out to explore interprofessional ethics, values,
and care relationships through a script-based narrative exercise.

The underlying premise of this elective is that strong teams
support patients, health professionals, and learners to engage
in the complex work of caring for individuals and families in
crisis. The workshop brings together a diverse group of staff and
students to explore patients' stories of care, professional roles,
values and ethics and ways to work effectively with patient partners in interprofessional collaborative teams.

The script unfolds as a series of dramatic narrative vignettes
dealing with issues such as the impact of diagnosis, treatments,
impact of illness on the patient and their family, and communication problems with health care providers. It raises difficult
and often unspoken challenges facing patients such as feeling
overwhelmed, afraid, and guilty. The script also highlights some
of the dilemmas faced by practitioners such as feeling helpless
and needing support from team members.

This elective is unique for several reasons, including participation by both students and practicing health care providers from
within the hospitals (UHN and Women's College Hospital) and
the use of readers' theatre. Students and staff learning together
interprofessionally sends a powerful message for everyone that
interprofessional learning is truly lifelong learning, as we are never
"finished" IPE—there is always more to learn. Using readers' theatre
is a powerful technique that transforms the script from something
that is read silently to oneself to something more akin to radio
theatre play in which the performance is only heard. Volunteers
from the audience are invited to the front of the room to read their
assigned role aloud for the entire group. The range of perspectives
this approach brings is remarkable for those both listening to, and
speaking the words of, a patient/health care provider.

The session ends with a debriefing , when the entire room
works together to make meaning of what has been heard, sharing reflections and questions. A critical part of this experience
has been the careful facilitation in which key interprofessional
learning moments are identified and elevated, and participants
are asked to reflect specifically on the value of their interprofessional learning and discussion. For example, they may be asked,

"What was the value of hearing firsthand how the professional perspectives we each brought informed what we heard and what resonated most strongly with us?"

The narrative approach opens up potential for different kinds of conversations about practice and professional identity. The use of patient stories as the basis for focused questioning effectively builds a sense of joint responsibility for ethical decision making, excellent patient care, and reflective, respectful practice.

CASE STUDY 8
Critical Perspectives in Global Health

OFFERED FOR THE FIRST TIME IN 2013, THIS ELECTIVE WAS CREATED to capture the growing numbers of international health placements and the focus on interprofessional education at the U of T. An interprofessional group from nursing, occupational therapy, physical therapy, and speech-language pathology drew from a pre-existing course in the Faculty of Nursing, "Critical Perspectives in Global Health," which is a mandatory course for nursing students taking international placements over the summer term.

The original nursing course focuses on global citizenship; introduces critical, feminist, and postcolonial concepts to students; and explores issues of professionalism in the context of North-South inequities. It offers students in the nursing program an explicit guiding concept of nursing practice that focuses on intensive preparatory sessions as essential to successful international placements.

The IPE elective builds on this course, adapting four of the six preparatory sessions to prepare students from different health professions for an international clinical experience. It engages the students with a broad range of global health issues and collaborative practice as well as sessions that cover IPE, Collaborative Practice and Core Concepts in Global Health, Ethical Considerations, Infectious Disease (with focus on tuberculosis) and Non Communicable Diseases (NCDs), and personal safety abroad.

Freida Chavez, lead for this elective from the Faculty of Nursing, says, "It's been a great exercise to work through with colleagues what content is meaningful to all health science students on an overseas placement. I think the course and the student learning will be better by incorporating a team approach where it really fits and taking a nursing approach where that is most appropriate. It has been a really good process, and we've all learned so much."

CASE STUDY 9
Infant and Child Oral Health Promotion

AN INNOVATIVE LEARNING ACTIVITY HAS BEEN DEVELOPED BY Professor Gajanan Kulkarni as the first dentistry-led elective in the IPE curriculum. This is the only IPE activity that has dentistry and young children as its focus. The learning objectives of this elective are primarily to educate the participating health science professional program students on the concepts of optimal oral health in children from infancy onward, emphasizing the unique contributions they can make in their respective professional practices. This three-hour IPE learning activity provides students with practical knowledge and skills regarding oral health promotion for infants and young children in a community setting. Students learn communication skills that enable them to competently counsel parents regarding the maintenance of good oral health for their child, right from birth. Following a brief session overview, students watch an oral health promotion video and observe a pediatric dentist perform an oral exam with an infant and mother. Students are then divided into groups and engage in small group discussions based on four typical clinical cases that highlight the most common preventable oral problems in children. Students are presented with typical case histories and questions arising from them. Each group presents their responses to the questions to the entire group, with responses being moderated by Dr. Kulkarni. Results from the first three sessions have shown that this oral health promotion IPE learning activity is very well received and effective in providing students with the knowledge, skills/ behaviours, and attitudes to be future participants in a collaborative health strategy targeting this area.

"Given the age group of the participating students, it is an activity which has not only benefits as a student of one of the health professions, but as a young parent to be. This IPE activity is unique in that it will impact both the students' professional as well as personal lives."

– Gajanan Kulkarni, Dentistry at U of T

Creating a Standard of Quality for IPE

To attend to the challenge of ensuring consistency of learning experiences for students within the curriculum, a working group under the auspices of the IFCC created the Points for Interprofessional Education System (PIPES). PIPES acts as a quality framework by providing scores for each existing and potential IPE learning activity to ensure a standard level of quality. To satisfy the minimum quality requirements, all applications for recognition of potential learning activities are scored on four process and four content criteria.

The points system also allows for the categorization of learning activities in the IPE curriculum, which aids in ensuring that the core competencies are covered and the requirements of the IPE curriculum completed. Development of PIPES in 2008 took place in two phases. The first step was to develop a consensus on the criteria across all programs. To achieve this consensus, a modified and international two-stage Delphi technique was used to develop a list of the key components of an IPE session. After this, the working group developed the points system. Criteria were ranked and distilled; eight criteria were selected for inclusion in PIPES, which were then divided into two different categories: process and content. Four criteria in the process category focus on how the learning occurs within the learning activity, and four content criteria reflect the structure of the activity.

Thus, equal weight was given to the process of learning as to the content. Within the system, each elective learning activity receives an allocation of points based on PIPES criteria: two process and two content criteria must be present for each activity, with a minimum of **ten process**, **ten content**, and thirty points overall accrued to become an endorsed IPE learning activity within the curriculum.

Through a rigorous approach, a consensus was established concerning the curriculum components required to achieve competency and skill in interprofessional practice. The IFCC was then able to move quickly to the challenging task of negotiating priorities and space in the health professions curricula at U of T. Importantly, it was the very act of developing the consensus around the framework that built the capacity for further work.

Points Allocation

Process (How)

P1 - Level of IP interactivity

P2 - Number of professions with IPE educated facilitators

P3 - Number of professions represented in student participants

P4 - Frequency of interactions across the learning activity

Content (What)

C1 - Realistic and authentic IP learning activity (performance-based)

C2 - Explicit IPE learning outcomes—number of IPE constructs

C3 - Debrief period with students and facilitators after IPE learning activity

C4 - Case-based learning

Figure 10—PIPES chart

0	5	10	Number
Didactic	Discussion	Interactive	
1	2	>2	
<3	3	>3	
1	2	≥3	
		Process Sub-Total	
See/hear	Talk/Dialogue	Do/Real Life	
1	2	3	
None	Informal debrief: reflection focusing on content	Facilitated debrief: reflection focusing on content and process (guidelines provided)	
No cases	Case presentation with some application (adjunct to learning activity)	Dedicated case presentation and in-depth dialogue (primary focus of learning activity)	
		Content Sub-Total	
		Total Learning Activity Points	

*http://www.ipe.
utoronto.ca/std/
docs/1.2_PIPEs_
Information_
Package.pdf*

NOTE: To be incorporated into the IPE curriculum, each learning activity must have two process and two content criteria. In addition, a minimum of 10 process, 10 content and 30 points overall must be accrued.

© Centre for Interprofessional Education, University of Toronto

Reflection Questions: Building the Curriculum

These reflection questions provide a starting point for those interested in building an IPE/C curriculum at their institution.

1. What competencies will anchor your IPE/C program?

2. Do curricula already exist that align with the competencies of your IPE/C program? Might elements of these curricula be adapted for IPE/C purposes? Are new learning activities needed?

3. What strategies will you develop to integrate your IPE/C program into profession-specific curricula?

4. How will the quality of IPE learning experiences be determined?

5. At what stages of the students' programs will IPE be introduced?

6. How will student learning be assessed?

7. How will the success of the IPE program be evaluated?

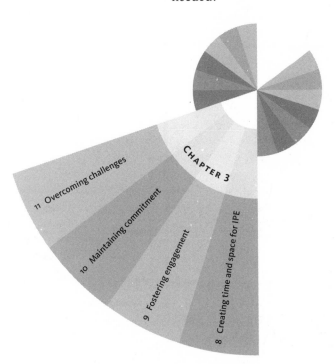

CHAPTER 4

Creating a Strong Education–Practice Interface

D EVELOPING STRENGTH AT THE PRACTICE–EDUCATION INTER-
face is of critical importance for interprofessional education (IPE) to succeed in any system or organization.
Everyone knows that even the best-designed educational program can be wiped away if students enter a practice setting in
which the "hidden curriculum" contradicts the theories and
skills they have been taught. Students need to see a positive
attitude to interprofessional collaboration and directly and
personally experience the benefits of team-based practice. It
is difficult to overstate the importance of the culture of institutions in which students learn to become clinicians. The
most robust interprofessional curricula, faculty policies, and
leadership development on the university side will come to
naught if students, on entering clinical practice settings, see
nothing that enables them to take up a new kind of practice
that is interprofessional and driven by patient/client, rather
than professional, needs. Faced with powerful mentors who
teach the opposite of what is taught in the education setting,
siloed practice will persist.

An important principle underpinning the Toronto Model
is that the university and clinical practice sites are not two
solitudes. Gone are the days when students first spent long
years learning basic sciences in a knowledge-heavy, class-
room-based curriculum before moving over to entirely practical, preceptor-based training in hospitals. Instead, twenty-
first century health professional curricula are characterized by
integration—weaving together acquiring new knowledge with
learning new skills. Today's health professional students are
often exposed to practice settings in their first months. Learning takes place in a wide variety of settings, both real and
virtual, in universities and colleges, in hospitals and clinics,

in the community, and, increasingly, in cyberspace. Breaking down the walls that have traditionally separated classroom and patient care is of great benefit to interprofessional education because it tightens the link between learning and practice. It also means that health care professionals who work in hospitals increasingly are taking on roles as teachers and mentors—roles that place additional demands on their skills and commitment to education. Clinical practice settings are not passive recipients of students on "placements" but rather are part of a dynamic educational system that provides teaching and role modeling, which significantly shapes attitudes and future behaviours of students.

In recent years all health care institutions, including hospitals, have become more and more interested in interprofessional practice and team-based care. As discussed in Chapter 2, this change stems in large part from an emerging literature linking these newer ways of practicing to better patient outcomes. Hospitals are also collecting more and more data on patient care outcomes, patient satisfaction, and patient-centred care. In the process, it has become apparent that health professional students are also part of health care teams, and thus it is important that their practices align with hospital best practices. Hospitals' interest in interprofessional care (IPC) coincides with a rise in interest in IPE in academic programs; the two combine to create a virtuous circle, each reinforcing the other.

In Toronto, leaders in teaching hospitals are not naïve about the magnitude of this shift in attitudes and practice, and they recognize that interprofessional and team-based care have been better established and practiced in some clinics, units, and clinical services than others. This makes it particularly important that the relationship between the university and their faculty members with the teachers and mentors in the clinical settings is close, reciprocal, and responsive. The Toronto Academic Health Science Network (TAHSN) has a close and productive relationship with the University of Toronto (U of T), other educational institutions, and all of the clinical practice settings and hospitals. But that close relationship is based on more than goodwill; it is based on a set of structures, clearly defined roles, and a commitment to evaluate—and, when necessary, adapt—the rules of engagement.

"If we do what we've always done, we'll get what we've always had. If we want something different, we have to prepare people to work differently. And that comes back to education."

– Sioban Nelson, Nursing at U of T

By 2007, the U of T was actively creating these structures, such as the Interfaculty Curriculum Committee (IFCC), to support and advance IPE; however, at the time there was no formal governance structure to do the same on the hospital side. Because the intent was to create IPE that would span the classroom to the clinical learning environment, the challenge was to formalize structures to oversee and integrate clinical placements within the hospitals and other clinical communities. Paradoxically perhaps, the IPE movement helped shine a light on the lack of dialogue between the university and the hospitals and the importance of new structures, such as a Centre for IPE, that could span both the university and the clinical environments.

"The rate at which new knowledge is being generated has grown exponentially in the last 25 years. No one clinician can know everything. By working together, we have the ability to build a team that is mightier than each of its parts."

– Emily Lap Sum Musing, executive director of Pharmacy at University Health Network

To move IPE forward in Toronto, it was necessary to do so in both the university and clinical settings—clinical settings that often included hospitals but also family practices, public health units, and other health care delivery settings. This need for clinical learning required U of T faculty members to partner with the clinical settings and to establish a joint governance structure for the Centre for IPE. Today there are effective lines of communication between university academic departments and faculties and clinical settings, something that greatly facilitates making changes needed to support IPE. Universities do not have authority over the hospitals and other clinical settings in Toronto, so a partnership is not only desirable but indispensable if IPE is to advance.

This chapter examines those structures and roles. A series of ten vignettes and mini-case studies provided by teaching hospitals and clinics in TAHSN demonstrates the wide range of ways clinicians and hospitals can build innovative programs to foster the spirit of interprofessionalism and interprofessional practice. Far from being something that ends when students leave the classroom, interprofessional education is intertwined with interprofessional care in ways that make them inseparable for students, but also for their teachers. Among the teaching hospitals in Toronto, different approaches were taken to optimize the interprofessional movement. This difference is illustrated in the chapter's three sections:

1. **Building the Structures and Roles to Support IPE/C** (Toronto Rehabilitation Institute, Sunnybrook Health Sciences Centre, St. Michael's Hospital, and Toronto East General Hospital)

2. **Developing Leaders, Teachers, and Mentors** (*ehpic*™ course and Collaborative Change Leadership program from the Centre for IPE; cases from North York General Hospital, St. Joseph's Health Centre, and The Hospital for Sick Children)

3. **Developing Innovative, Interprofessional Clinical Programs to Support IPE/C** (Holland Bloorview Kids Rehabilitation Hospital, Baycrest Centre for Geriatric Care, the Centre for Addiction and Mental Health, Mount Sinai Hospital, and the student-run IMAGINE clinic)

Overall, it's a story about developing critical mass. It is about seizing the opportunity and the chance to redefine what the teaching hospitals are and to define them as learning institutions that are true partners of the university—institutions that care about and focus on interprofessional, collaborative, patient-centred care as a way of learning and a way of practicing.

1. BUILDING THE STRUCTURES AND ROLES TO SUPPORT IPE/C

Interprofessional education is not an add-on. It requires a significant investment in time, resources, and the development of leaders and teachers in order to succeed. This section explores the infrastructure and resources that are necessary in practice settings to support the development of a next generation of health professionals who will value and engage in interprofessional, patient-centered practice and team-based care.

It is important to consider history. For hundreds of years, hospitals have been organized along disciplinary lines, staffed by professionals who worked in and were governed in professional silos. Today, commensurate with a new focus on interprofessional practice, there is a need to adopt interprofessional organizational and governance models. Educational re-

> "I think that if we're going to provide publicly-funded health care that provides the sort of care that our patients are looking for, it has to be in the context of interprofessional teamwork and we're committed to that."
>
> – Bob Bell, President and CEO, UHN

sources, support programs for teachers and students, and the physical resources and spaces necessary for teaching and learning must now run across and through the old unidisciplinary terrains, breaking down the silos of the past that sequestered education into separate edifices. It is vital that the two largest professions (medicine and nursing), which for so long were divided into separate monoliths, come together with other health professions so that the more than twenty different kinds of health professional students who populate health care institutions are not left stranded when those two giants have left the table. Several Toronto hospitals have found innovative ways to begin this journey and keep everyone on board.

One of the first Toronto hospitals to grapple with new organizational structures was the Toronto Rehabilitation Institute (Toronto Rehab), now part of the University Health Network. As an early adopter of IPE/C, Toronto Rehab had been experimenting with models of organization as well as educational development for over a decade. Lynne Sinclair, Innovative Program and External Development Lead at the Centre for IPE, took the first step in developing IPE placements (that would later become the fourth core learning activity in the requisite IPE curriculum for all health science students: the IPE Component in a Clinical Placement) by conducting a literature review, drawing on the lessons she and the Toronto Rehab team gleaned from the Canadian North, where the population is so sparse that one tiny outpost can provide health care for an entire region. "In Canada's rural and remote areas, clinicians really need to band and work together," she says. "These practitioners have a long history of interprofessional care."

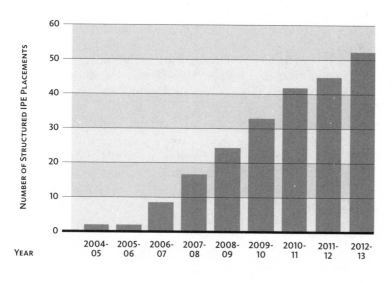

Figure 11—Number of Structured IPE Placements across Toronto Hospitals.

"Use this model as a template, but make it your own."

— Lynne Sinclair, Physical Therapy at U of T, Innovative Program and External Development lead

By 2004, Sinclair was ready to roll out the first structured IPE pilot placement in Toronto at Toronto Rehab. She, along with a team of educators, drew together six U of T students from the nursing, occupational therapy, pharmacy, physical therapy, social work, and speech-language pathology departments/faculties. They held tutorials so the students could get to know each other and come together as a team, and to facilitate the students' understanding of group dynamics. Then, students were scheduled for a four-week placement at the facility's geriatric day hospital. During the placement, Sinclair and colleagues met with the students once a week to encourage each student to share his or her profession's perspective on the clients they were working with in the day hospital.

The crowning moment for the pilot project came when the students walked into the hospital's lecture theatre to share enthusiastically the insights they had gained from their IPE experience. The presentation attracted more than fifty staff members, and a reporter from *Hospital News*, a Canadian health care newspaper, took photos and wrote about the event. "That's when my phone started ringing," recalls Sinclair. "Staff and other hospital leaders called to say, 'I wasn't trained this way. How can I learn this?' And all of a sudden, it just started to build. The presentation spurred a lot of energy for IPE."

Of course, there are always resisters to change. As Toronto Rehab was enjoying the successes of its first IPE experience, a chief nursing executive (CNE) at another acute-care hospital stated that she couldn't understand the need for IPE. Three years later, in 2007, the CNE, who held the hospital's education portfolio, was persuaded to allow an IPE pilot group of eight students to do a placement at her hospital. "The pilot placement was a way of getting a foot in the door," relates Sinclair. When the CNE attended the students' presentation, Sinclair says, "It was like a light bulb went off in her head. Leaders can hear the collaborative care message from us, but it's different when they hear it from students. Students relate the important point that they now understand their role in the system and who can work with them to achieve their patients' goals." And soon after, the CNE was busy creating a part-time IPE leadership position at her facility.

One unexpected outcome of the program was the way interprofessional education boosted recruitment and retention to practice sites. Because of the IPE experience, after gradua-

tion about half of the students involved in the Toronto Rehab pilot project accepted jobs at the same hospital. "The students wanted to practice in a facility where IPE is valued," explains Sinclair. At a time when staff shortages were threatening to paralyze health care in the province of Ontario, IPE was attracting applicants. "Today most health centres in the city have an IPE leader," says Sinclair.

Sharing the learning from these early experiences at Toronto Rehab and all that has resulted since across the IPE/C system has always been part of the Toronto program's philosophy. For example, a manual outlining the steps to establish IPE placements was made freely available online, and hundreds of academic teaching hospitals and family practice clinics have downloaded the free toolkit from the U of T Centre for IPE website.[1] The toolkit, "Facilitating Interprofessional Clinical Learning: Interprofessional Education Placements and other Opportunities," was funded by the Ontario Ministry of Health and Long Term Care's Interprofessional Mentoring, Preceptorship, Leadership, and Coaching (IMPLC) Fund (for details see Chapter 2). Of the many free online resources available through the Centre for IPE's website, this has been the most popular; over 200 individuals and organizations from around the world have accessed it. Developed by Toronto Rehab in partnership with the Office of IPE, this comprehensive 138-page guide was designed to help clinical settings plan and prepare staff and teams for structured IPE placements. It provides information and resources for leading and coordinating structured IPE placements. The guide is filled with practical strategies and tools for hosting structured IPE placements, leading workshops on IPE facilitator skills (including curriculum that can use the partner resource, an educational DVD on "Facilitating Interprofessional Collaboration with Students"), and evaluating placements. In addition to providing ideas for other types of interprofessional clinical learning opportunities, the toolkit contains an annotated list of key websites and published articles on IPE/C. That such a resource would be developed in a hospital illustrates the deep commitment of the institution to IPE. It also demonstrated, when it first appeared, that Toronto Rehab was serious about being a partner with the university in leading change.

http://www.stjoe.
on.ca/education/
pdf/Enhancing%20
IP%20Practice%20
Resource%20
Manual%20-%20
Part%201%20
of%203.pdf

"From a pharmacist's point of view, it's valuable to be part of the patient's admission, hospital stay and discharge, along with the physician, nurse and social worker. Collaboration between team members allows me to streamline patient care."

– Catherine Goulding, clinical pharmacist at Mount Sinai Hospital

While the whole manual is recommended, two dimensions of the manual are explored in more detail in this book. The first is the taxonomy of roles that institutions need to develop in order to host structured IPE placements specifically (see below). Some of these roles (e.g., IPE Leader) are critical to developing a robust program in IPE/C generally as well; that is, they support not only the experience of learners but also enable practitioners to develop their team functioning and collaborative skills.

The link between supporting practice education and clinical practice is foundational to the model developed at Toronto Rehab. The model for structured placements requires that students from different professions take part in facilitated tutorials over a four- to five-week period, each grounded in a clinical practice setting. The facilitation is different from the usual student placements. Two health professionals from different disciplines co-facilitate the sessions, allowing the students to drive the IPE placement curriculum as the group gets to know one another better. Facilitators model IPE in practice, supported by tutorials that are less about the specific content of the clinical practice area and more about interprofessional relationships and competencies.

A second model for the IPE Component in a Clinical Placement is the "flexible learning activity," a concept pioneered by Toronto Rehab and Centre for IPE leaders including Lynne Sinclair and Mandy Lowe, director of Educational Development at UHN and associate director at the Centre for IPE, and subsequently taken up across the Toronto network and beyond. Flexible learning activities were designed to build on approaches to interprofessional learning that were already widely used across practice settings. As Lowe describes, "We also didn't want to give the impression that interprofessional collaboration and education could only happen when large teams sit around a table. Interprofessional learning can happen between as few as two different providers exchanging questions, reflections, and information; it really depends on the practice context." Approaches that would enable and support learning explicitly from an interprofessional perspective were needed. This is what the flexible activities provided by fo-

> "Interprofessionalism requires constantly changing work strategies, hierarchies and power dynamics. People who are good at collaborating are able to tolerate not being the centre of attention. They have the ability to lead and, importantly, the ability to be led and *not* lead."
>
> – Brian Hodges, vice-president of Education at UHN

cusing on unique interprofessional learning objectives, posing questions that prompt interprofessional learning, and guiding reflection uniquely directed toward rich interprofessional learning.

As with any change, educational and institutional change is all about people. There are key roles that need to be played to ensure success in IPE in clinical practice settings. First and foremost, senior leaders must value, and be on record endorsing the value of, IPE and the centrality of interprofessional care. In Toronto many hospital CEOs take this stance. Additionally, Toronto hospitals have an organizational structure—relatively unique in Canada—that includes hospital VPs of education, many of whom also carry the torch for IPE/C. Support from senior management creates conditions of possibility for the individual roles described below to have meaning and profile in the institution.

Of pivotal importance is the identification of an individual who will hold an educational leadership role with the mandate to initiate, enhance, and support the integration of IPE into clinical disciplines in the hospital or practice setting. A variety of roles are necessary for the successful integration of IPE into an organization: these include a dedicated IPE leader, a team of IPE co-facilitators, clinical teachers, and other academic faculty members. It also requires administrative support such as program service/unit managers, support from one or more leaders of the institution's senior leadership, and, of course, the support of students and patients/families. Below are descriptions of some of these roles and their functions, derived from the Toronto Rehab manual. Of course, the structures and needs of each institution are different, and roles should be adapted for each specific context. The roles described below are the ones we have found useful. They anchor interprofessional education to interprofessional care, and they support both the university and the service providers' goals of improving care and training the next generation of health care professionals to work effectively together.

The role descriptions below are uniquely positioned to support IPE in clinical settings, such as the structured IPE placements and flexible learning activities.

KEY ROLES IN IPE IMPLEMENTATION

An **IPE leader** coordinates the planning of placements, including determining which placement opportunities can be offered, and liaises with the various academic faculties participating. The leader orients, educates, and coaches clinical teachers and faculty members to IPE placement philosophy, goals, and pro-

cesses, and orients students to the same elements, with the assistance of specific placement IPE facilitators. The leader plays a key role in supporting the IPE facilitators, clinical teachers, and faculty members in their roles, and leads the development and evaluation of the IPE placement program. This role can be constructed in several ways, the most desirable being a full-time position dedicated to the development and facilitation of IPE. A full-time IPE leader can work directly with the vice president or director of Education in a hospital or health care organization and with deans of the various faculties and health professional schools. The IPE leader will be involved in all aspects of the development, coordination, implementation, and evaluation of the IPE program. They can also oversee the development of a teacher/faculty development program. Some institutions will elect to have a part-time leader (for example 0.5 FTE) to lead all aspects of the IPE Placement program and Clinical Faculty Development programs, or perhaps a leader with 0.2 FTE time to simply report directly to the vice president or director of Education about the coordination of the IPE placement program within the institution. The depth and complexity of activities undertaken will depend on the size of the institution and the resources available to support the role. However, we have found that institutions that appointed an IPE leader with a substantial portion of time dedicated to the IPE role have had greater success than those who appoint an individual who has many other responsibilities and who therefore can dedicate only a minor part of their time to IPE.

Measures of success for an IPE leader might include:

- number of IPE placements;
- number of IPE learning opportunities offered for all students in a particular kind of placement;
- development or implementation of a teacher/faculty development program;
- presentations on the organization's IPE initiatives to administrative or academic audiences;
- securing funding for educational research from external agencies; and
- publications.

Since the creation of the first IPE lead role at Toronto Rehab, there are now IPE leadership roles across all of the Toronto hospitals. It has been interesting and significant to note a shift from a focus on the leaders of IPE in the beginning to roles that reflect greater integration of both IPE and IPC perhaps because in such integrated leadership roles, it is easier

to address the interprofessional priorities of both students and staff in practice settings.

IPE co-facilitators work together with the IPE leader to coordinate introductory materials as well as patient-themed tutorials during placements. They meet with IPE clinical teachers and faculty members to orient them to the goals and objectives of the placements, and review program content prior to working with students. While students are onsite, these co-facilitators support their interprofessional learning through weekly tutorials and a student team presentation on a topic of relevance to the clinical setting.

Clinical teachers play a crucial role in the success of IPE placements and must understand IPE philosophy, goals, and processes. Because they will act in supervisory and evaluative roles, their expressed attitudes and role modeling are of prime importance. They provide content expertise as necessary for group tutorials, support the IPE process as a whole, and set the tone for IPE and its importance to clinical practice in the institution.

A *program service* or *unit manager* plays a key role in identifying clinical teams interested in hosting IPE placements, supporting interested teachers and faculty members, liaising with the IPE leaders and co-facilitators, and working to build an interprofessional education culture.

Patients/clients provide a critical component to IPE. Their engagement in IPE education and training initiatives is critical to keeping the focus on patient care and undermining the tendencies of the professions to think that this effort is all about them.

Students/learners play a vital role in the success of IPE. Their participation ranges from working together to identify shared interprofessional learning objectives, sharing their learning freely with group members, collaborating in a joint project, and providing feedback to continuously improve interprofessional learning opportunities.

A *sponsor* at the institution's senior leadership level is invaluable to champion the IPE model, to align institutional priorities with IPE activities, to provide support and encouragement to the IPE leader, and to disseminate

> "Interprofessional education started out with a few people whispering their vision of health professionals learning together. Then IPE began to happen, and the vision became louder and louder. Now IPE is embedded in everything. And in the future IPE will become the standard."
>
> – Dante Morra, chief of staff,
>   Trillium Health Partners

evaluation data about IPE activities in the institution.

The IPE leads at Toronto Rehab and members of the Centre for IPE played a crucial coaching role across all the teaching hospital sites. In addition to providing a wide range of supporting materials (e.g., manual, DVD, professional/faculty development programs), early on-site coaching enabled a small, expert team from Toronto Rehab and the Centre for IPE to collaborate with key leaders (including the hospital's senior leadership, Education leaders, and IPE leader) to support them in developing IPE programs. They also assisted the hospitals to tailor the material and approaches to their own unique contexts.

All of these players need to work in concert to develop an integrated community of practice. Strategies need to be developed to ensure that key players function in a coordinated way and that lines of communication are clear within a given organization and across the health care system. Creating such a structure is illustrated by the case of IPE at Sunnybrook Health Sciences Centre, a large academic health sciences centre in mid-Toronto. In 2008, a grassroots group of health professionals at Sunnybrook started talking seriously about interprofessional education. Using ideas gleaned from faculty development courses (described later in this chapter) and supported by the Centre for IPE and the Toronto Rehab team, they piloted their first structured placement. This model of teaching was quite a departure from traditional clinical rotations/placements and needed a new set of academic structures to be in place. To do this, an Interprofessional Education Committee (IPE Committee) was formed in early 2009. The first task was for committee members to learn about each other's professions as well as the educational requirements for the students in various professions. For many, this was the first such conversation. However, commonalities soon appeared, and it was clear that the professions shared many of the same issues about clinical education. Exploring these issues together provided an opportunity for members to work with colleagues who they otherwise might have never even met. Because the IPE structured placements were new for everyone at Sunnybrook, there was a need to collectively develop infrastructure and capacity and to deal with the daunting prospect of facilitating a group of students from different professions.

Key factors in moving forward were the calm and supportive IPE facilitators who could help clinicians take on a "new" task that was not part of their job description. This task involved the creation of a common student calendar to help determine the best blocks for scheduling placements and to deal

with room bookings and schedules with flexibility. Since the first pilot in 2008, Sunnybrook has now hosted an impressive total of thirty-three such structured placements in the clinical areas such as Palliative Care, Women and Babies, Emergency, Burns, Oncology, General Medicine, Trauma, Critical Care, Gerontology, Mental Health, Long Term Care, Musculoskeletal Care, Internal Medicine, and Patient and Family Support. Over two hundred students from twenty-two different regulated and unregulated health professions have participated. The training of over sixty IPE facilitators has supported the program, and the original IPE Committee has welcomed members of additional health professions.

Students and facilitators alike find this to be a positive experience, and today Sunnybrook clinical staff request to become involved in IPE placements. Students and facilitators receive a certificate for their professional portfolios, and thank you letters are always copied to the managers. Energy and enthusiasm for IPE is spreading throughout the organization as a result of this program, and IPE at Sunnybrook is no longer limited to a small group of early adopters.

In addition to defining roles and creating oversight committees, there is also a need to consider what physical spaces support IPE. St. Michael's Hospital in Toronto focused on creating a place for all of their learners to transform the student experience from uniprofessional to an interprofessional experience. Educators at St. Michael's became aware that where learners go—to find information, to have lunch, to put their coats, to study, and to access learning resources—is of paramount importance to students. They were also aware that these experiences reflect on the organization as a whole and its desirability as a place of eventual employment. The way in which physical resources and spaces are organized conveys volumes about the institution, its identity, and its hierarchies.

The opportunity to advance the hospital's IPE goals came at a time when St. Michael's was making a major commitment to research, knowledge translation, and education. The Li Ka Shing International Healthcare Education Centre would became one of the first facilities in Toronto to embody a truly interprofessional space for its students. Originally, St. Michael's had embarked on a campaign to create a research tower, with traditional training programs attached to research labs. In 2008, however, the opportunity to apply for funds from the Li Ka Shing Foundation changed those plans and put a focus on knowledge translation; the research tower proposal evolved to become an education and research center. At the same time, the hospital was engaging in a strategic plan that focused on the quality of student experience, and an education summit was

held to which students were invited. Asking the students what they thought was important brought one resounding answer: space. "One thing was clear," says Patricia Houston, VP Education. "Students wanted space to learn together." The hospital listened. So struck were hospital leaders by the strength of the student feedback that they decided not to wait for the new space but to create an integrated Student Centre within their existing space as a temporary measure.

Today at St. Michael's Hospital, teaching is closely aligned with research and care. "St. Michael's is a teaching hospital," says Rob Fox, the hospital's vice president of Planning and Development, "and it wasn't hard to explain to the board how this project aligned with the priorities of the hospital." Houston championed the proposal, as did the CEO, Robert Howard, who had previously held the position of VP Education and firmly believed excellence in education was a core mission of the hospital. Everything came together at once, resulting in the creation of unparalleled space and opportunity for IPE at St. Michael's Hospital.

When the integrated Student Centre first opened in the fall of 2009, it was an immediate success. The Student Centre provided "touch-down" space for students, including lounges and locker rooms, but also provided centralized access to the administrative side of student placements. The co-location of **staff and faculty** involved in education, irrespective of discipline, was key. Just by sharing the space, staff and faculty began to take an integrated, collective, and student-focused approach. Through co-location they began to learn about each other's programs, all finding much more in common than they had anticipated. By the time the purpose built education and research tower opened in November 2011, the Student Centre team had crystalized into a consolidated group that was able to collectively have input into the new facility's look and function.

Today, *all* students in placements at St. Michael's Hospital see the same team. "This has been transformative," says Houston. "We think of the students now as one body, rather than consider each discipline individually. Many students have questions regarding placements that aren't necessarily discipline-specific—now, we can help students faster in a team-based environment." It's been such a success, and the students feel so supported, that the Student Centre team was awarded the Centre for IPE's Award of Merit for Excellence in Interprofessional Education Teaching (Team) in 2012.

The evolution of an integrated Student Centre has had many positive spin-offs for the hospital. For example, a collaborative point-of-care educational team embarked on a campaign to

educate about and assess hand washing. This was made much easier by working with a fully interprofessional team, including doctors, medical fellows, nurses, families, and patients, all of whom engaged in the campaign together. Further, the Student Centre has developed an online learning portal: "MyLearning" provides a place for all learners, regardless of profession, and it advances IPE at the hospital by allowing learners to develop their educational experiences through an IPE lens. The software is so popular that other hospitals in Toronto are purchasing licenses for use in their own facilities. The creation of the Student Centre at St. Michael's was a product of innovative thought, external funding, and, most important, champions at senior executive levels within the hospital. Patricia Houston recalls, "It fit the vision of St Mike's. We all knew it was a great idea. No one needed a lot of convincing."

CASE STUDY
St. Michael's Hospital: Student Experience Committee

IN 2012, THE STUDENT EXPERIENCE COMMITTEE (SEC) AT ST. MIchael's Hospital received the Award of Merit for Excellence in Interprofessional Education (Team) from the Centre for IPE at the University of Toronto. The SEC oversees the activities of the Student Centre, constructed as part of the Li Ka Shing Knowledge Institute in 2011. The Student Centre is home to all the administrative coordinators from the respective educational programs with placements at the hospital. Bringing these administrators together improves the placement experience for all students at St. Michael's by consolidating resources and expertise of all of the administrators. The SEC also oversaw the development of a common Student Registration System that allows for tailored and efficient on-boarding of each student. Coupled with the Student Registration System is a web-based orientation that is both comprehensive to the hospital and individualized for each student.

The SEC also supports IPE curricular programming, such as the Student Centre IPE Lunch Series and the Student Café. The IPE Lunch Series is a structured presentation given by an individ-

> "I felt like an employee, not like a student, because of the good level of access to the library, student area, participation in rounds, etc. St. Michael's has a very good environment for students and it is conducive to student learning."
>
> – Comment from Student Engagement Survey

ual or team on a specific IPE topic, and it has monthly enrolment of approximately eighteen. The Student Café is an interactive program where students, faculty, and administrative leads meet monthly to discuss complex issues they may have encountered, such as breaking bad news or hospice care.

The SEC at St. Michael's believes in living the philosophy of interprofessionalism. The Student Centre is a place for students from all disciplines, and the students feel embraced by the organization.

Case Study,
Toronto East General Partnership Councils

Toronto East General Hospital "partnership councils" are part of the shared governance structure at the hospital and another example of enhancing collaborative teams through intentional structures. Partnership councils are interprofessional bodies with the purpose of influencing organizational decision making through representation of those people most directly involved in the provision of care. The membership of each partnership council represents the professional and occupational diversity of each unit, offering an interprofessional forum for dialogue about the things that matter most in the hospital's day-to-day work.

A compelling example comes from the maternal/newborn partnership council. This council's members—in this instance the key groups involved were nurses, lactation consultants, social workers, spiritual care, and housekeeping—found themselves reflecting on an experience they had on the unit following a stillbirth. The clinical staff had made the decision to leave the family alone with their baby, giving time for the extended family to arrive and grieve with the new parents. Then, however, the communication system efficiently but mechanically did what it was designed to do; the family was officially recorded as "discharged." This step initiated a request to the facilities services staff to come and clean the room. As a result, a member of facilities staff stepped into a highly emotional and private family experience, not realizing what had just transpired. On reflection, the partnership council understood that this was an unintended event that was not in the best interests of the family, nor of the staff member who had unintentionally intruded in a deeply personal and painful moment.

The council wrestled with this scenario, recognizing that they could do better by patients, family members, and team members. Several members of the council looked to other organizations, diverse cultures, and bodies of literature for strategies that would avoid a similar situation. One council member came

upon the image of a butterfly, recognizing that in many cultures it serves as a metaphor for transformation. Working with the communications department, infection control, printing departments, clinicians, and management, the council developed a strategy to post a discreet picture of a butterfly on the door of any patient or family that requires privacy. The strategy has since spread through the hospital, such that all staff members know that any closed door with the image of a butterfly represents a moment of transformation. While the context of that moment might be different for each patient and family, the image itself evokes a sacred space not to be intruded upon. It was through interprofessional dialogue, the willingness to reflect, and an orientation to systems thinking that allowed this partnership council to have a lasting influence on the experience of care for patients and families.

2. DEVELOPING LEADERS, TEACHERS, AND MENTORS

Establishing a favorable institutional IPE culture evolves from an organizational commitment to interprofessional practice and to the creation of leadership roles, structures, and physical spaces as described above. But it also rests on an institutional commitment to the education and development of people: leaders, teachers, and mentors. This means that institutions have to attend to and evaluate education as a component of the work of clinical staff. The centerpiece of this work in Toronto has been the creation of the "Educating Health Professionals in Interprofessional Care" (*ehpic*™) course that was created for IPE faculty, clinicians, and leaders across the Toronto network.

ehpic™

The *ehpic*™ course originated in 2004 through a CanMEDS research and development grant from the Royal College of Physicians and Surgeons of Canada. The initial pilot, led by Ivy Oandasan, was a thirty-nine-hour certificate course implemented in 2005 for University of Toronto health professional educational leaders from twelve faculties/departments. The course aimed to develop academic leaders in IPE who would acquire the knowledge, skills, and attitudes to teach both learners and fellow colleagues the art and science of working collaboratively for patient-centred care. The course has evolved over the years and has now been offered across Canada and the United States, as well as in Denmark, Australia and Saudi Arabia; the program now has over one thousand graduates. It has also been

provided in truncated formats through workshops, seminars, and three-day courses. The week-long version of the program has garnered accolades both in Toronto and internationally, and according to Mandy Lowe, the current *ehpic*™ course director and associate director of U of T's Centre for IPE, the program often has a waiting list. "It's intended for those who have a role of influence," explains Lowe.

"Ultimately it's about building a better system," adds Maria Tassone, the director of the Centre for IPE. "The people who enroll in *ehpic*™ are system-thinking people; they have a worldview. They care about education and about improving care." Participants in *ehpic*™ are both academic educators and clinicians, underscoring that IPE cuts across the continuum of learning and strengthens the partnerships between university and practice settings. Applicants to *ehpic*™ are asked to send in a 250-word abstract of the interprofessional initiative they want to undertake, describing how the knowledge they gain from the course will assist their team in moving the project forward. "Ideally, the whole team working on the project enrolls in *ehpic*™," says Lowe, who is also the director of Education and Professional Development at University Health Network, a four-hospital organization. "The strength of the program is that we don't just talk about interprofessionalism; the participants immediately apply the principles they learn to their project. The course is very experiential, from beginning to end."

After the abstracts are reviewed to ensure the fit between interprofessional learning and the proposed initiative, participants are notified of their acceptance or asked to further clarify how their initiative can move toward becoming more interprofessional. Participants are then invited to formally

ehpic™ Alumnus View

"At Indiana University, we hosted the *ehpic*™ conference in April 2012. This conference, from the course content to the expert facilitators, is simply a 'must do' for any university or health system that is invested in furthering their development in the area of interprofessional education and collaborative practice. The Centre for Interprofessional Education at the University of Toronto offers external content expertise, an impressive bibliography of IPE scholarship, and facilitators that are energetic, professional, and up to date. We were most impressed by the willingness of the *ehpic*™ course facilitators to truly 'customize' the course for the needs of the host organization. As an example, we had specific goals for faculty development that we wanted the *ehpic*™ facilitators to address and they did not disappoint! At the conclusion of each day of the course, the

register, a process that includes completing a learning needs assessment and reflective essay about IPE and their hopes for participation in the program. All of this information informs the faculty (facilitators) who lead the curriculum. It is critical that faculty have a clear sense of what the priorities are for each group of participants because each group is different and affords unique opportunities to tailor teaching and learning. The participant group membership may vary, for example, in terms of the balance of academic faculty or clinical leaders from practice settings; types of professions and roles; and international or local participants. These and many other pieces of information inform the faculty as they develop curriculum for that specific iteration of the course. "As a faculty, we start meeting at least six to seven months prior to the five-day course each June. We focus not only on the logistics but also on tailoring the course and our own faculty development. This last part is critical for us as life-long interprofessional learners and educators … What are we learning or do we need to learn to incorporate into our teaching specifically?" says Lowe.

When the forty to sixty registrants arrive at the *ehpic*™ course, they're each handed a workbook—which measures almost two inches thick—that includes learning exercises and a variety of resources on interprofessionalism. Then they're assigned a table. "Every table has six to eight participants, and they're seated to maximize the diversity of professions and roles," explains Lowe. Soon, the registrants are engaging in an interprofessional icebreaker designed to get them talking and learning about each other and the professions represented at their table. For example, one icebreaker begins: Tell the story about when you decided to become a member of

facilitators met with our planning team to make real-time adjustments to the next day's course content and events. We can say with confidence, that the *ehpic*™ course was a catalyst for positive change at our institution and was integral to the formation of our recently created Center for Interprofessional Education and Practice. If you are a host organization considering the *ehpic*™ course... do not hesitate to bring their team to you. They are worth the investment and you will not be disappointed."

– Lee Wilbur, Associate Director for Curriculum Implementation,
   Center for Interprofessional Education and Practice

your health care profession/role. As the exercise progresses, participants learn not only about each other's personal history but also about their current role. One of the key learnings participants often cite during this exercise is recognition of what they hold in common, such as similar motivations for their work in helping others.

The curriculum is designed to build on the learning of each day," explains Lowe. "For example, we support learners to fully participate in an interprofessional facilitation simulation by the end of day three (of the five-day course). But this is carefully developed so the learning builds; after learning about group dynamics and interprofessional facilitation theory and research, participants will then analyze group dynamics and facilitation in interprofessional teams using video vignettes to stimulate discussion. From there, the participants are asked to reflect on their own competencies for interprofessional facilitation and learn about best practices in briefing and debriefing a simulation before role playing a simulated patient discharge meeting to practice interprofessional facilitation skills. Afterward, they'll not only reflect on their interprofessional collaboration and the team dynamics that were at play, but on the learning associated with the facilitation process itself.

Each day, time is allotted for the participants to reflect on their learning and to apply what they learned to their plans for interprofessional initiatives at home. Initiatives can range from new IPE curriculum at a college or university in areas such as quality, safety, or simulation to novel interprofessional orientation programs for new staff within practice settings to faculty development programs that build local capacity for IPE and IPC. Participants also have opportunities to share their initiatives with the others, enabling them to draw insights from the community of participants.

The five-day format requires more than ten facilitators, including faculty from multiple professional programs and one or more guest speakers who are people who have experienced firsthand the impact of varying degrees of interprofessional care on their own health and well-being. The guest speaker(s) are a critical part of *ehpic*™ that brings the true and deeply personal impact of interprofessional care to the conversation. This portion of the course is highly valued by participants, many of whom go on to replicate the use of narratives in their own work back home.

The faculty for the program is a rich mix of old and new hands—collectively combining experience with new ideas and perspectives each year. Two to four of the faculty members are primary leads of the curriculum each day. The faculty co-facilitate and may also operate much like a tag team, taking

turns running activities and leading discussions. Of critical importance is the role modeling of interprofessional collaboration among the faculty (this is frequently cited by participants as very enabling of their learning, too). For example, although only a subgroup of faculty may lead a particular module in *ehpic*™, there are core leads (e.g., director, administrative lead) who are present each day to ensure continuity and flow. Facilitator debriefings also occur throughout and at the end of each day to ensure sharing of key learnings from the group and seamless facilitation that enables optimal interprofessional learning for participants.

Two or three months after the course, the participants are required to submit their reflections on what they learned at *ehpic*™ as well as an essay on how they are applying their learning to their interprofessional initiative at home. A facilitator provides individualized feedback, and after participants submit their essay they receive an official certificate. There are now graduates of the *ehpic*™ course across Canada, and many are leading changes in their own provinces, including Universities of British Columbia, Manitoba, Saskatchewan, Alberta, and Calgary as well as colleges and universities across Ontario. Hundreds of graduates are also spread across the United States and internationally, where they have been inspired to lead transformation in their home institutions.

In Toronto, one offshoot program took IPE development to a mastery level by giving teachers and faculty members the opportunity to develop and lead IPE projects of their own. North York General Hospital (NYGH) is a community academic hospital in the Toronto network that aims to "lead the pursuit of excellence through learning, innovation, and partnerships." In operationalizing this goal, NYGH embedded a focus on IPE. After attending the *ehpic*™ course, NYGH leaders returned to the hospital and developed their own program, called iPed (Interprofessional Education Development). Consisting initially of four 90-minute workshops over four consecutive months, sessions were developed and facilitated by a team of educators to include principles of IPE and reflective practice, collaboration and teamwork, IPE facilitation, conflict resolution, and feedback. The program was a complete departure from previous education programs at the hospital. However, since the launch of iPed, three courses have been offered with more than seventy-five participants from twelve professions.

While NYGH continues to build capacity in IPE, it has not been without challenges. Great care was taken to involve physicians and to achieve a healthy balance of staff in the program (which has tended to have higher representation by nurses). Sustainability of the program has also been a challenge.

However, NYGH has recently recruited an IPE leader for the program and continues to offer iPed, with many of its graduates now participating as facilitators. The hospital relies on the success of iPed for its IPE efforts and shares its knowledge locally, nationally, and internationally.

Susan Woollard, director of Medicine and Eldercare, and Rick Penciner, director of Medical Education, NYGH, recount that students who participate in iPed consistently report enhanced self-awareness and use of reflection in team settings, the promotion of active involvement and engagement in teams, and an enhanced ability to identify and manage conflict. Overall Woollard and Penciner see the impact at the organizational level: "We continue to build capacity in IPE at NYGH. We believe that much of this is attributed to iPed—both directly and indirectly. Some of the course "graduates" have now participated as facilitators in our IPE student-structured placements. Two more interprofessional teams have now participated in the leadership course on interprofessional collaboration at University of Toronto. It's wonderful to see this program continue to grow and IPE/C build at the hospital."

COLLABORATIVE CHANGE LEADERSHIP

As the critical mass of *ehpic*™ graduates grew and IPE took root in Toronto and beyond, the need to develop people who could lead within and across complex contexts and continue to build momentum and culture change toward interprofessionalism was identified. This is the goal of the Collaborative Change Leadership program, an intensive program for leaders and future leaders that runs over the course of a year. The Collaborative Change Leadership program (CCL) is a certificate program for health care and health education leaders. Originally funded by the Ministry of Health and Long-Term Care's Interprofessional Education and Care Fund in 2009, and led through the University Health Network and the Centre for IPE, the CCL brings together leading educators and health service leaders on a focused program of leadership development. In a robust program evaluation, graduates emphasize the transformative and empowering nature of the experience, and the year-long change projects that participants undertake over the course of the program have had a major impact on the sponsoring organizations and the health care system as a whole. As individual leaders, they have developed capacities to ask more learner-oriented questions, reflect more deeply on their leadership practices, sense more effectively the needs within their systems, and model collaboration in all they do. Learnings from this program

will contribute to the development of a pan-Canadian program on collaborative leadership as part of the Canadian Interprofessional Health Leadership Collaborative described in Chapter 5.

In addition to *ehpic*™ and CCL, the Centre for IPE continues to develop new opportunities for learning to address emerging community and system needs, often in collaboration

Collaborative Change Leadership Program Summary

Session	Session Focus	Between-Session Expectations
Session 1 Discovering What Is	Exploring change theories and leadership practices; setting up a capstone project and organizational inquiry; initiating community of practice.	Pre-reading before session 1. Between sessions 1 and 2, conduct organizational inquiry and participate in peer coaching; assigned readings.
Session 2 Imagining the Possibilities	Interpreting organizational inquiry results, deepening knowledge of emergent change and meaning making; begin designing change strategies and evaluation.	Between sessions 2 & 3, work with collaborative partners to co-design draft change strategy; work with assigned faculty coach.
Session 3 Designing & Implementing	Navigating the tension between implementing a change plan and sensing system needs and adapting accordingly; leading meaning and making processes.	Between sessions 3 & 4, begin implementation of change strategy in organization, with coaching from faculty. Peer-coaching within community of practice.
Session 4 Sensing, Evaluating and Adapting	Assessing movement, reflection and adapting strategies based on what is emerging as meaningful in the organization.	Continue implementing and adapting change initiatives; coaching within community of practice and with faculty.
Session 5 Accomplishments, Reflection, and Adaptation	Presenting and celebrating work and coaching each other; assessing movement, reflecting on and adapting strategies based on what is emerging as meaningful in the organization and the system.	

with key partners. For example, the Centre for IPE partnered with service providers Bridgepoint Health and Surrey Place to create "Clicking Collaboratively," a workshop designed to build skills in interprofessional facilitation that is online as opposed to face to face. Another recent example of new partnerships is a two-day workshop called "Synergies," which is about the interface of IPE and simulation and is co-led by the Centre for IPE and SIM-one, a not-for-profit organization that connects the simulation community, facilities, resources, and services across the province of Ontario.

"It helped me to see my role as a change leader and the toolkit I can call upon to help me with my journey."

"This course went well beyond any expectations I had. Having recently completed a Master's program and comparing this course with some of those—I have been surprised that this course is hands down better than many of those courses."

"For those who have an interest in learning how to stimulate change within their health care organizations, and who want to use a different approach to identifying and planning future initiatives that will make a difference in their organizations, this program provides all the necessary ingredients."

– CCL Program Participants

CASE STUDY
St. Joseph's Health Centre:
Team Coaching in Health Care Settings

COACHING AND TRAINING POINT-OF-CARE HEALTH PROFESSIONALS to develop expertise in IPE and collaborative care is a key element in developing champions of practice change, but is also necessary to develop skilled teachers for the IPE curriculum. At St. Joseph's Health Centre, a community teaching hospital in the west end of Toronto, each of the clinical unit-based point of care teams were given an opportunity to participate in six hours of visioning and enabling workshops related to collaboration and IPE. Through the project Enhancing Interprofessional Practice through Team Coaching in Healthcare Settings[2] a train-the-trainer model was used as a way of "developing more than thirty expert 'team coaches' who worked with our teams to facilitate conversations and goal setting around collaborative practice," explains Elizabeth McLaney, director of Interprofessional Education and Collaboration at St. Joseph's. Adopting appreciative inquiry—a strengths-based approach to change that originated in health care—as the theoretical basis for the workshops, the conversations focused around five core competencies for collaboration:

- trust and respect
- knowledge of roles
- appreciating differences and conflict resolution
- willingness to share power
- shared decision making

Following the workshops, participants reported substantial change in four dimensions of the five. Trust was established as already being high for most teams, and no significant changes were noted following the workshops. There were, however significant changes in teams' knowledge of each other's roles and their abilities to resolve conflict after the workshops, but the two areas where there was the most change were power sharing and shared decision making (both significant changes). "This was a very important finding for us and reinforced the importance of conducting these or similar activities," said McLaney.

By taking the time to engage in reflective activities, create a shared vision, and generate action plans focused on collaboration, the teams reported that the workshops "created some space" for people to interact who normally would not have an opportunity to come together. Other feedback was that the program built friendships and collaboration on an emotional and personal level. With regard to power sharing, participants noted "at the first session

all the leadership people sat at one table and all the staff sat at another—at the next meeting people were intermingled."

But how long did the effect of the workshops last? McLaney reports that when they revisited the teams six months to a year after the workshops, they reported many outstanding examples of how they had enhanced team collaboration. For instance, following the workshops, the neonatal intensive care unit (NICU) team started up monthly Interprofessional Education Rounds. They realized they had not previously invited their pharmacist to team meetings. They also invited a lactation consultant from the community to collaborate with their team. The renal team created a Patient and Family Council, bringing together patients and families to meet regularly with the team, and also began to include their registration clerk at meetings. The inpatient surgical team created an interprofessional orientation for surgical residents and developed a pharmacy information board to enhance team communication. The take-home message from this intervention was clear: with a small amount of dedicated time and with the internal expertise of team coaches, Point of Care Teams realized a synergy whereby they increased their collaboration and created concrete outcomes in how they worked together—and worked with patients and families.

If one observes well-functioning teams, it is clear that the team members have a shared sense of purpose and that they trust each other. They model an understanding of and respect for each other's professional and personal strengths and limitations, and they can articulate confidence in each other's ability to achieve the team's goals. Effective teams share an understanding of group/team norms and help the team to be inclusive. But even well-functioning teams can be supported to get even better through ongoing focus on team development.

To a great degree, these cultural elements of well-functioning teams arise from effective leadership. Effective team leaders have personal credibility and are individuals who know how to communicate regularly and clearly with their team members. They are able to involve all team members, and they encourage them to develop their skills and potential. They are able to help the team manage change and to lead a review of goals and objectives as necessary. They ensure team members are accountable and complete assigned tasks. In more mature teams, leadership can be shared, with different team members being able (and allowed) to take on responsibility for specific tasks, according to the skills and competencies they possess and the demands of the task.

Clinical teams need to have explicit processes for the issues they face in health care, such as attending to problems as they arise, managing and navigating through conflict, evaluating the performance of individuals and the team, and reviewing health team

program goals and planning. The case studies that follow outline some of the ways in which hospitals are specifically developing their teams to be as effective and patient centred as possible.

CASE STUDY
*Hospital for Sick Children
Partnered Learning Project*

WITH SUPPORT FROM THE MINISTRY OF HEALTH AND LONG-TERM Care, Lorelei Lingard and her team at The Hospital for Sick Children partnered with colleagues at Toronto Rehab and the Children's Hospital of Eastern Ontario in a Partnered Learning Project (PLP). Over an eighteen-month period across these three sites, interprofessional practice was promoted through team training and student placements. The purpose of the project was threefold: (1) to increase interprofessional collaboration capacity in staff and students; (2) to gather descriptive data, providing insight into the processes of interprofessional collaboration and interprofessional education (IPE); and (3) to describe some early outcomes of these experiences. The PLP focused on enhancing the capacity for interprofessional collaboration of both clinical teams and health care students on placement. Separate learning activities were designed and implemented for each group.

Interprofessional collaboration concepts and language to better enable team members to support student IPE learning during their placement were introduced to clinical teams through workshops, with the goal of increasing awareness of each team's own collaborative practice. The workshops were interactive, using role play and standardized patients. Once the teams completed the training, they hosted an interprofessional student placement whereby students from different disciplines were placed together. During the placement, students participated in weekly IPE tutorials led by specially trained IPE facilitators.

Bonnie Fleming Carroll, associate chief of Nursing and IPE at The Hospital for Sick Children, described the project as enormously successful for all participants. "Students felt they

"Open lines of communication and an understanding of the responsibilities of each discipline allow members of any discipline to report the positive or adverse effects of medications to the pharmacist who can then process and suggest changes, if necessary. This is of great importance because it ensures that no one person is responsible for our patients – we all have a hand in their care."

– Virginia Fernandes, clinical pharmacist
at Mount Sinai Hospital

learned about each other's roles, the value of communication between professionals, and increased their confidence in asking about others' roles. Preceptors had no doubt the students benefitted, and many commented on the benefits they too experienced whereby having students enrolled in the IPE program prompted them to personally reflect more on their own roles and collaborative practices." Best of all, at the end of the program, all sites had successfully increased staff capacity in interprofessional collaboration and education, and they were able to offer more IPE placements for learners as a result.

3. Developing Innovative, Interprofessional Clinical Programs to Support IPE/C

In addition to leadership training and capacity building, many hospitals in Toronto have engaged in rethinking the way care is delivered in clinical practice settings in order to support IPE and IPC. For Holland Bloorview Kids Rehabilitation Hospital, Canada's largest pediatric rehabilitation center that provides programs and services for children and youth with a variety of disabilities, the development of a structured IPE clinical placement for learners was an experience that allowed them to live their mission of being client- and family-centred by integrating family members as teachers and facilitators of student learning.

Holland Bloorview is a leader in the inclusion of clients and families as key members of the interprofessional team. Its well-developed collaborative care environment supports the active participation of clients and families in all aspects of their care. Taking this philosophy to heart, Holland Bloorview built its IPE clinical placement around families and clients. They began by inviting clients and families to share their stories and perspectives during IPE placement tutorial sessions. This preliminary engagement of clients and families in IPE sessions resulted in enthusiastic feedback from both the learners and the educators. The clients and families appreciated the opportunity to connect directly with learners and enjoyed interacting with a wide range of students and educators. They took very seriously the chance to influence the students' appreciation for the importance of collaboration in health care.

The success of this early process led the IPE leader in collaboration with the director of the Family Leadership Program to take a purposeful look at family involvement in IPE activities and IPE facilitation training. The family and client feedback, the student enthusiasm, and the obvious success of the strategy of getting families and clients to teach collaborative interprofessional care led to the development of a program where-

*http://partnered
learningproject.ca*

by families are now integral to IPE at Holland Bloorview and involved in the planning and delivery of all IPE sessions. As the program evolved, Holland Bloorview provided formal training for clients and families for their roles as educators, advisors, and mentors through the family leadership program.

Patient Educator Crystal Chin has been part of this evolution. A former client at Holland Bloorview, Chin began by volunteering to work with young clients while she was a teenager. She recalls how, as she got older, her goals changed. She is now enthusiastic about fostering collaborative culture in health care that is beneficial to patients and families. She works primarily with adolescent patients and brings the perspective of youth to multiple programs within the hospital. Chin completed training as family faculty and undertook a family leadership program. She has found that one of the important roles patient educators play is to help health professional students understand the multiple perspectives of patients. She emphasizes the great difference between communication with the parents of young children and communicating with adolescents. Health care providers in pediatrics need to be able to do both if they are going to effectively engage families and youth in their plan of care. Coaching students on how to avoid acronyms and emphasizing the importance of removing redundancy and duplication among team members are the topics covered in Chin's lunchtime sessions with students. As a former Holland Bloorview client who has now transitioned into the adult sector, Chin finds clinicians in adult care more territorial and less collaborative. She believes that it is somewhat easier in pediatrics because family involvement is so important.

Chin sees the current emphasis on IPE/C as an important development. "It puts a label on it and creates it as a focus for health care. I believe it is very positive, as it recognized everyone has to work together. Health care specializations are atomic but the human body is holistic, encompassing everything from physical symptoms to social determinants of health. It takes a team to bring that perspective to health care." Chin is also part of a program that brings a family perspective to research at Holland Bloorview to ensure all proposed studies have the potential to make a positive contribution to families and patients in their community.

Other innovations that have flowed from the patient faculty initiative include a new program to engage clients and families in the development and enactment of simulations that involve critical conversation among clients, parents, and team members. Darlene Hubley, IPE leader at Holland Bloorview, explains, "The simulations will be available for staff and students and will provide opportunity for dialogue to further

the understanding of the family and client perspective as the pivotal member of the collaborative care team." Dr. Golda Milo-Manson, VP Medicine and Academic Affairs, adds, "We are very proud that IPE has led to an increase in family and client engagement at Holland Bloorview. The students love the engagement, and it models family-centred care. It's a great outcome for everyone."

Beginning with a small pilot project offered summer of 2007, the success of the family leadership program at Holland Bloorview led to the creation of a full IPE program. This organization is now an enthusiastic proponent of IPE, offering a clinical environment that supports students to obtain flexible IPE credits, an IPE program that offers formal structured IPE clinical placements, IPE lunch-and-learn sessions, and IPE seminars. In addition IPE facilitators who have been trained at Holland Bloorview are active participants as patient volunteers and faculty in IPE activities at the University of Toronto and also participate in multiple interorganizational, collaborative IPE projects across TAHSN and U of T.

One initiative in interprofessional education, this time in the long-term care (LTC) sector, is an innovative arts-based learning project designed to enhance the self-reflection skills of learners. At Baycrest Centre for Geriatric Care, ten student interns from a variety of disciplines worked with a skilled facilitator and professional artist interacting with residents in an arts program. As one intern commented, "Art can act as a venue for communication and can assist with getting to know, not just the resident, but each other." The results of this project informed further arts-based approaches to engage LTC home staff, students, and residents by learning with, from, and about each other. Jennifer Reguindin, interprofessional educator for Baycrest, believes there are many opportunities to improve care in LTC settings through interprofessional initiatives. "Starting with specific gerontological competency development, followed by inter-provider training, we feel that IPE provides a much needed framework to open the conversation concerning resident- and family-centred care in the LTC sector."

A similar transformation is underway at Toronto's Centre for Addiction and Mental Health (CAMH), a psychiatric teaching hospital serving a large and diverse urban population. In 2012 CAMH launched its eight-year strategic plan, "Vision 2020: tomorrow, today." Of the six strategic directions, one is a commitment to enhance recovery by improving access to integrated care and social support. In the past, members of the care team worked independently of one another, and there was sometimes a lack of clarity about the scope of each other's practice. Professional jargon resulted in disjointed care plans. Today, em-

bedding a recovery-oriented practice model of care within high-functioning interprofessional psychiatric teams is a large step forward for care—and for education.

A key feature of mental health teams is the inclusion of paraprofessionals: peer support workers, family, community members, or client advocates. Different members of diverse teams are skilled at screening and assessment, diagnosis and psychopharmacology, treatment planning and monitoring process, crisis intervention and de-escalation, motivational interviewing, skills development and psychoeducation, housing and income support systems, and knowledge of community resources. By getting to know how each member of the team will approach the problem, the treatment, and the specific modalities they will use, students have the opportunity to learn with and from the team and each other to maximize treatment outcomes. Exposing students to this process both enhances their future ability to work collaboratively and helps foster a positive attitude to collaborative models of care.

Today CAMH combines clinical care, research, education, policy development, and health promotion in an interprofessional way to help transform the lives of people affected by mental health and addiction issues. Since 2010, an occupational therapist and social worker have designed, developed, and delivered an educational program for staff that embeds the concepts of interprofessional collaboration within the context of a recovery-oriented model of care. Involving case workers, nursing, occupational therapy, peer support workers, psychology, recreational therapy, and social work in the program, the facilitators utilize a blended learning model that combines didactic, small-group activities and large-group discussions, guest speakers, online learning modules, and community visits spanning a six-week period. During weeks 1 to 4 participants attend a four-hour session supported by online tutorials and quizzes. Topics included: clinician assumptions and biases about mental health and recovery; hope; managing health/illness; and empowerment. During the fifth week, participants visit a community mental health agency. During the final week, participants report back on their community visits and have the opportunity to discuss what they learned during the course. In this way, participants develop the ability to describe the roles and responsibilities of the various members of the team; acquire

> **"The fact that [we're] meeting physicians who are in their 50s who weren't educated in an interprofessional environment so they might not know what other roles are… we actually help educate those people."**
>
> – Nikki Fischer, medical student

and utilize the concepts of interprofessional care to enhance team cohesion and functioning; integrate an interprofessional team approach within a recovery-oriented practice model of care; apply the knowledge and skills in the day-to-day care of clients; and discover agencies and services in the community congruent with the recovery-oriented practice model of care.

CASE STUDY
Mount Sinai Hospital Team Check-Ins

TAKING THE APPROACH THAT SPACE, TIME, AND INTENT ARE KEY FAC-tors in creating effective teams, some of the strategies used at Mount Sinai Hospital (MSH) include weekly interprofessional team meetings, weekday staff/patient meetings, shared interprofessional participation clinical encounters, and "team check-ins" on the inpatient psychiatry unit. Team check-ins are an innovation designed to support collaboration within health care teams. When participating in a check-in, individual team members are encouraged to ask themselves questions about whether team members are being heard and respected, what is enabling/supporting collaboration, whether or not there is anything interfering with the ability of members of the team to contribute meaningfully, and what might be done to improve team interaction. Not every question is answered every day, but the questions serve as touch-points that allow the team to improve their function collectively.

In the experience of Donna Romano, nursing unit administrator, Department of Psychiatry, and IPE Coordinator at Mount Sinai Hospital, patients and their families may experience additional distress when the members of their interprofessional team do not effectively communicate. "The patients know when team members are not effectively collaborating and communicating. Patients can face many challenges being in hospital and coping with their illness experience. We owe it to them to be as seamless and succinct about the treatment we are able to provide."

"Interprofessionalism is not only about the everyday business of providing clinical care, it is also about attention to team process. It's about doing a self-assessment as a team. There are three questions we can ask at a team check-in: How did we do today as a team? Were team members heard and respected? Is there anything that would have improved our team interaction?" Adopting this approach has helped the inpatient psychiatry unit at MSH to maintain high staff retention and satisfaction as well as high patient ratings of quality of care and service received. In fact, team check-ins were highlighted during Mount Sinai Hospital's 2012 Accreditation Canada cycle.

The development of IPE placements has also served as an impetus to developing an awareness of collaborative team practice within organizations and has provided the opportunity to support the development of team-based care. Getting the right placements for students is a challenge because of the problem of ensuring that there are appropriate role models in each clinical setting. The Hospital for Sick Children decided to tackle this tricky issue by using the structured IPE placement as a way to introduce an awareness of team competencies to clinical teams. The impetus was student learning, but the benefits could flow both ways—to team members and to learners. The Partnered Learning Project (PLP) set out to advance both IPE and team competence.

CASE STUDY
Women's College Hospital
Intimate partner abuse: How is this relevant to me as a future health care provider?

WOMEN'S COLLEGE HOSPITAL, IN COLLABORATION WITH THE Rehab Sciences sector at U of T, has offered an elective on partner abuse and sexual assault since 2009, focused on responding effectively to interpersonal violence and its health impacts. The session is designed with interprofessional teamwork in mind, with small- and large-group discussions as well as content geared to providers' roles and clinical skills. In particular, there is a focus on identifying health and mental health impacts of violence, responding sensitively to disclosures, and increasing students' awareness of community resources.

This learning activity employs a number of pedagogical strategies using the story of "Jennifer," a case study concerning a student nearing the end of her placement who is concerned about a patient who has not returned for follow-up in an outpatient clinic. It is presented as an interactive skit that describes patient interactions with health care providers and includes interprofessional panels that highlight various professional roles. The content of the activity can also be tailored to the audience to make it as relevant as possible to day-to-day practice. For instance, when the team discovered a large group of pharmacy students was planning to attend, the scenario was adapted to include a

> "I always tell the students that by working as a team with each other and with the family and clients we are actually more efficient in pediatrics and we save the system money."
>
> – Crystal Chin, Patient Educator, Holland Bloorview Kids Rehabilitation Hospital

"IPE is a great way to learn about things from each other's perspectives in order to be successful in complex collaboration."

– Rani Srivastava, Vice President and Chief Nursing Executive, Centre for Addiction and Mental Health

discussion on how abusive partners may control their partners' medication.

Learning objectives for the session include creating a common clinical knowledge base as well as understanding the importance of interprofessional teamwork. Content includes: common myths about partner abuse, barriers to leaving abusive relationships, common indicators (or clinical "red flags"), and strategies for asking about the issue and responding nonjudgmentally. By working in small interprofessional groups, participants have succeeded in identifying common concerns. Building on the IPE icebreakers developed by the Centre for IPE (which begins the process of reflection and discussion on professional roles), the students are asked to introduce themselves and talk about any (formal) training they have received on this issue in their professional programs and whether they have had direct experience with this issue in clinical placements. This opens up an important discussion on the relevance of the issue across professional lines—as well as validating the sense that health care providers often feel ill-equipped to address this issue in practice. One of the highlights from the 2013 session was small-group discussion on cases drawn from clinical scenarios at the Sexual Assault/Domestic Violence Care Centre and the ensuing discussion facilitated by a forensic nurse on care planning and responding to patients' needs.

Many important themes regarding interprofessional care surface in this activity, including knowing the skills and expertise of people on your team, the importance of sharing both knowledge and responsibility for complex or high-risk situations, managing issues of confidentiality within the team related to care providers receiving different client disclosures, the role of documentation as a communication tool, having shared goals as a team to provide consistency in care, and the importance of meeting patients' medical, emotional, and psychosocial needs.

THE NEXT GENERATION OF HEALTH PROFESSIONALS IS PASSIONate about team-based care and changing the way health professionals practice. The Toronto IMAGINE (Interprofessional Medical and Allied Groups for Improving Neighbourhood Environments) clinic is a student initiative that perfectly encapsulates a new vision for health care and health care practice. It is a clinic for underserviced individuals creat-

ed and run entirely by students. It arose out of a recognition that building a culture of IPE rests on a parallel commitment to interprofessional, team-based care, and yet learners are sometimes frustrated that their formal curricular experiences are not always in line with this sentiment. In addition, IMAGINE was formed to address the health needs of marginalized groups in the community (i.e., people with precarious immigration status, experiencing homelessness, or without identification).

Since its inauguration in 2010, IMAGINE has not only served its local community but also improved the quality of education and practice of its many student volunteers. The IMAGINE website lists its first goal as "[to] promote interprofessional education," and this team-oriented mind frame permeates both the students and leaders of the clinic. "The clinic breaks down barriers between professions," said Yick Kan Cheung, one of two co-directors of IMAGINE. "The students work together; they get to see the dynamics of a health care team in action."

The clinic's team is composed of five students and five preceptors, from five health disciplines: physiotherapy, pharmacy, nursing, medicine, and social work. The students gather before the clinic's 10:00 a.m. opening for introductions and to discuss expectations and goals. The Clinic Operations team heads discussion. When asked what drew them to IMAGINE, most students agree that it is to gain experience on an interprofessional team, for practical clinical experience, or both. "On our busiest day we saw nine patients, including a bus full of Korean refugees," stated Mahwesh Siddiqi, one of two operations managers present. "It can get pretty overwhelming, but we just work as a team and divide the work."

As patients arrive, volunteers discuss which students should examine each patient. After initial assessment, students determine the best course of action for the patient as a team. Each participant's contribution is particular to his or her educational lens and experience. Together, they develop an appropriate plan for treatment. Social work volunteers, for example, offer input concerning referrals and long-term care, while physiotherapy volunteers brainstorm ideas for increasing mobility through exercises and assis-

> "Interprofessional collaboration capacity building can be accomplished through faculty development. Training facilitators to enable health care teams to function optimally is a model that can be disseminated widely."
>
> – Ivan Silver, Vice President Education, Centre for Addiction and Mental Health

tive devices to those in need. Pharmacy may explain to the group the importance of properly using an inhaler, and inefficacy resulting from incorrect use. "Each student has their own perspective—their own lens—through which they view a patient," said Enoch Ng, IMAGINE's co-director. "It's really helpful to both students and patients to combine those perspectives."

In addition to its Saturday clinic, IMAGINE boasts a wide array of community outreach events, including barbeques, lectures, and workshops with themes ranging from heart health and diabetes, to lice and bedbug prevention. "Part of what we do is create trust in the community," said Yick Kan Cheung. "Developing a presence through workshops and lectures informs people that we are here, and we are here to help." IMAGINE provides a platform through which students can experience an interprofessional team, learn skills that cannot be taught in a classroom, and give real care to real patients in need. Enoch Ng concludes, "You can teach most knowledge from a book, but you can't teach the things you learn here: empathy, compassion, and those kinds of values that are so important to health care." For Michael Bonares, a U of T medical student and volunteer at the IMAGINE clinic, the fact that all the teams students are exposed to outside of the IMAGINE Clinic don't demonstrate interprofessional practice is a concern: "I find practice is often more multidisciplinary than interdisciplinary. IPE is really good in theory, it just still has a long way to come practically." With a commitment to true interprofessional and team-based care in clinical settings, such as is practiced at the IMAGINE clinic,

IMAGINE: A Student's View

Jen Galle, medical resident, IMAGINE alumnus

"In my second year of medical school I became the IPE representative for the student governing council for the Faculty of Medicine at Toronto (MedSoc) student government. I got involved with a group of students who wanted to start an interprofessional workshop based out of a community health center and then actual student-led health care clinic. We ended up starting a workshop—every Saturday a group of students go into St. Christopher House—which is a community center at Bathurst and Queen Street West that has a lot of inner-city, homeless, and many aboriginal clients. A group of four students went and provided a workshop to clients on whatever they wanted to talk about. One week they wanted to learn about the liver and how it related to alcoholism, and the basics about the heart.

Those workshops evolved into IMAGINE, a weekly clinic, where students in teams of four (medicine, dentistry, social work, and nursing) provide care. Patients are triaged by a team member, and depending on the patient's problem, the students will go into one of the clinic rooms. The students are supported by four mentors who are health care professionals; these mentors run the critically important debriefing sessions at the end of the day.

learners will adopt the behaviours and attitudes that are needed for interprofessional practice.

CASE STUDY
Baycrest Creating Interprovider Models of Care

SINCE ITS INCEPTION IN THE FALL OF 2011, THE BAYCREST CENTRE FOR Learning, Research and Innovation (CLRI) in Long-Term Care has garnered international interest in its unique approach to interprofessional education. The Baycrest CLRI is one of three funded sites under a five-year program supported by the Government of Ontario to enhance the quality of seniors' care through education, research, innovation, evidence-based service delivery and design, and knowledge transfer. As part of this funding, the Baycrest CLRI is mandated to enhance interprofessional geriatric competencies in the long-term care home workforce, using innovative educational approaches. Housed on two levels of a 472-bed long-term care facility for the aged, the Baycrest CLRI represents the next generation "teaching nursing home" and includes interprovider learning units that serve not only students but staff from across the province as well. The use of the term "interprovider" stems from a recognition of the unique composition of a long-term care workforce that includes both regulated and unregulated care providers. Traditional techniques such as bedside teaching, combined with innovative strategies such as simulation, team-huddles, and arts-based learning will allow learners to experience real-time, hands-on learning.

The students in IMAGINE had to discuss issues like scope of practice, and how we envisioned the clinic from the perspective of each profession. First of all I learned what these different professions actually did and had to offer. This was something I would never have learned—certainly not in such detail—in a conventional medical education. Because you're working so closely with people, you establish relationships with people outside your profession. I found this to be really beneficial, especially as someone in medical school where you're seeing the same two hundred people every day. At IMAGINE we were meeting and working with people who are connected to you in health care but are not necessarily in medicine. That was really powerful.

It has had a big impact on me as a doctor. I recognize that other health care professions have expertise I don't have. For instance, I now know that if a patient came to me with a musculoskeletal issue they would likely benefit from PT [physical therapy] and strength training. My sister is a nurse. I see the education she's gone through. I don't know how to do a lot of the bedside things she does, particularly within hospital settings. Now, in the hospital I consult with the nurses and seek their input because they are the people who are with the patient for an extended time during the day, and I need to know what they know."

THE TORONTO ACADEMIC HEALTH SCIENCE NETWORK IS CHARacterized by its close, collegial relationships between the University of Toronto and its fully and partially affiliated teaching hospitals and clinics. As can be seen in the case studies described in this chapter, each hospital has taken its own pathway to interprofessional education and practice. Some have emphasized the creation of formal roles and structures; some the development of leaders, teachers, and mentors; and some have focused on changing the way they deliver clinical care. Each in its own way has been an important piece of the puzzle in moving the whole Toronto network toward interprofessional education. The collegial relationships among institutions has been important in fostering an openness to sharing ideas and innovations. Programs developed at one hospital are quickly taken up at others. Fostering this level of sharing, scaling up innovations, and providing support across the system has been a key role of the Centre for IPE. This has been achieved by sustaining a community of practice, developing a regular newsletter with a readership of thousands, and by intentionally bringing together groups of people who have no other means of connecting—through the IPE Clinical Leader Network and the Academic Coordinators of Clinical Education, for example. With this book, our intention is to share these innovations even more widely.

Perhaps the biggest barrier to developing IPE is what is sometimes called the "hidden curriculum." All the innovations in the world cannot, on their own, overcome the cognitive dissonance a student will experience when a respected clinical teacher speaks negatively about teamwork, collaboration, or the role of other health professionals. While the Toronto hospitals have attended to innovative structures, development of leaders and teachers, and new clinical practices, it is perhaps the shift to see IPE/C in a positive light—indeed, as an indispensable part of good patient- and family-centred care—that is most responsible for the success to date. Much remains to be done, and it would be an exaggeration to say that IPE has penetrated all corners of the Toronto Academic Health Sciences Network, but the spirit of IPE is alive and well in Toronto's clinical practice settings.

Reflection Questions: Creating a Strong Education–Practice Interface

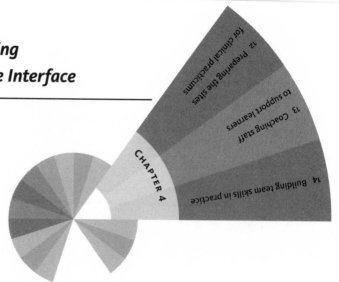

These reflection questions are designed to focus your attention on the links between the practice setting and the university.

1. What are the critical roles needed to design, implement, evaluate, and sustain your IPE/C in practice?

2. What IPE/C exemplars already exist in practice? How do you know they're exemplars?

3. How will you know that practice organizations are ready to engage in IPE/C?

4. How will you build and grow opportunities for authentic, practice-based learning experiences with real patients and real teams?

5. How will faculty (including clinical faculty) be developed, supported, and coached to teach, lead, and facilitate IPE? What are the key capabilities needed to teach, facilitate, and lead IPE in your system?

6. How will you attend to the "hidden curriculum" from an interprofessional perspective?

CHAPTER 5

Thinking about Impact and
Sustainability from the Start

A SK ANY OF THE EDUCATORS AND LEADERS IN HEALTH PROFES-
sional education (IPE) at the University of Toronto or
across the world, "What is the next big thing for interprofessional education?" and they will likely answer that IPE
must be embedded in the accreditation and assessment frameworks for health professional education by the certification
boards and the regulators. "All of the accreditation and certification bodies must include criteria that support interprofessionalism in their evaluation processes if IPE is to be taken
seriously and reinforced," states Brian Hodges, the vice president of Education at Toronto's University Health Network.

ACCREDITATION

In the area of accreditation in Canada, these moves are underway, with the accrediting bodies for six health care professions
already having introduced the requirement to show evidence
of IPE. "When the accrediting body says 'Thou shalt have an
interprofessional standard,' it advances IPE across the board,"
agrees Maria Tassone, director of the Centre for IPE.

"In undergraduate medicine, for example, the standards
are changing. An IPE standard is coming down the pipeline,"
says Jay Rosenfield, the vice dean of undergraduate medical
education at the University of Toronto (U of T). Early in 2013,
the Liaison Committee on Medical Education made the leap
into interprofessional training. They approved a new standard
that mandates all medical schools across the United States and
Canada include education with other health professionals as
part of medical training.

In Canada, postgraduate medical education has had to
fulfill the accreditation requirements of the Royal College of

HIGHLIGHTS

1 Accreditation
for education
programs and
service providers

2 Evaluation –
new directions

3 Competency in
interprofessional
education and
practice

Physicians and Surgeons of Canada CanMEDS competency framework and its "collaborator" role since 1996. When you consider that U of T has more than three thousand fellows and residents representing seventy-eight different specialties, meeting the IPE requirement seems formidable. The educators, though, have embraced the challenge and established a wide array of seminars, IPE toolkits, and online learning modules.

Former dean of Nursing and current vice-provost Academic Programs, Sioban Nelson agrees with the push for accreditation: "For many schools, accreditation is the only means they have to garner resources from within their institution to ensure that IPE is supported by the universities." These days many schools and programs are fighting to keep up with the burgeoning essential components of their curricula. For IPE to survive tough times and competing demands in the education sector, it has to be core and mandated.

Although there is strong consensus that accreditation is the future, however, there are many different views concerning the detail. Opinions vary as to which competencies are most important, what should be part of accreditation, and who should have a say in the content and the process. The U of T's competency framework, which is widely cited and a major influence around the world, is subject to the same debates. For instance, one issue that Tassone feels passionate about is the need to strengthen the leadership competency at the entry-to-practice level. "We still mix up management and leadership," she says. "What we want are collaborative leaders who can make decisions based on the wisdom of many people in their team and organization, who can engage with diverse perspectives. In politics, I see a lot of singular charismatic leaders, but we need to move away from that model. Shared leadership doesn't sit with one person; it sits in a collective way. And that's a bit radical."

Other educators believe the thirty competencies in the U of T model (see Figure 7) still aren't enough to capture the skills needed by the interprofessional team player. Salvatore Spadafora, the vice dean of Postgraduate Medical Education at U of T, suggests adding a new competency: *resilience*. "We need to tell our learners that they will make mistakes," he says. "Part of teaching resilience is teaching that crow must be eaten warm. You make a mistake and you need to catch it quickly, reflect on it, and go and say, 'I shouldn't have behaved that way and I need to apologize. I was an awful person, and there is no excuse for it even though I was stressed, tired, hungry and had fourteen things going on at home.' If you can do that, you'll be resilient."

Still others at U of T would like to flip the IPE competencies upside-down as part of a massive curriculum overhaul
in which health care consumers drive the competencies. "The
public wants all health care providers—nurses or doctors or
social workers or pharmacists or dentists—to be compassion-
ate," says Sarita Verma, the deputy dean of U of T's Faculty of
Medicine. "They want them to have empathy, to be generous
with their time, to be patient, to be tolerant, to be humble
enough to ask when they don't know."

In fact, Verma believes accreditation standards need much
more than the addition of an IPE requirement. "Curriculum
is developed by the academics and tested by the regulatory
credentialing bodies, and in all that process the public is not
engaged," she says. "Standards should be developed in consultation with the public and with the patient population. They
should be informed by community engagement." Verma also
thinks that the accrediting bodies can perpetuate the boundaries that separate the professions. "I find there is a very
deep-seated mentality of tribalism among the specialties," she
says. "There's a guild mentality of self-protection under the
guise of accreditation standards and regulation."

Nelson thinks communication skills are the priority but laments that these are not given the primacy they deserve by accreditors. "We should be reviewed on how we teach and how
students perform on communication skills—communication
with colleagues, with patients and families, and with staff and
members of the public in general." According to Nelson, "At
the moment this is taught with varying degrees of intensity
across the programs. It is not taught interprofessionally, and
yet it is key to equipping students to successfully negotiating
the inevitable challenges of health care practice and the good
and bad team communication they will encounter throughout
their careers."

Spadafora, an anesthesiologist, takes a similar view and
challenges educators to ground the students' development of
IPE competencies in everyday reality. "We are training our
learners to work in the Garden of Eden. They're doing rotations and electives that are IPE and IPC based, and we're
doing our roles well and communicating well, and, yes, it's
important to model that. But have we exposed them to multiple contexts of practice and experiences that are *not* positive? I'm not suggesting that we find someone who is an ogre
and throw our young to him, but we need a system in which
learners can have a bad experience and then debrief about it.
What we don't want are learners blaming their team members
or putting labels on them. Our team members are our valued
colleagues. It doesn't bring us up by bringing them down."

ASSESSMENT

The other driving force for change is student assessment of learning. While accreditation is the process that drives the behaviour of institutions, assessment drives the behaviour of students. It is widely acknowledged that the assessment of interprofessional competence must run deeper; it must penetrate placements that are not specifically part of the IPE curriculum. The above-mentioned CanMEDS framework for medical residents, for example, mandates the assessment of collaboration skills on all clinical rotations. We are a long way from realizing this sort of pervasive assessment of IPE skills and competencies. However, many professions are adopting tools that make room for a wide range of professional input into assessment. Multisource feedback, also called 360-degree evaluation, for example, is becoming more common. Some programs in Toronto seek the feedback of many different health professionals in the practice assessment of clinical learners. While much more needs to be done, simply undertaking such an assessment sends a powerful message.

Interprofessional education is still new, and everyone wants to take a good look at it. Beyond the conversation about accreditation, hospital administrators, faculty, and clinicians are examining it closely, peppering the advocates with questions. Does IPE influence practice? Does it lead to efficiencies? Will it save health care dollars? The burning question, though, is: Does IPE improve patient health outcomes? The World Health Organization's (WHO) 2010 "Framework for Action on Interprofessional Education and Collaborative Practice," proclaims that collaborative practice can decrease everything from the need for hospital admissions, total client complications, length of hospital stay, and clinical error rates.

Most experts are more constrained in their claims. "People want to see a return on their investment," explains Tassone. "There's pressure to show that IPE goes straight to improving patient outcomes, and that's the conundrum because it isn't possible to show a linear relationship. The evaluation work that speaks to the impact of IPE has not yet been done. There isn't a conceptual theory of what the impact of IPE would look like, and until that time we struggle to think of how to frame, let alone measure, impact." Scott Reeves, formerly at U of T and now heading up the Center for Innovation in Interprofessional Education, University of California, San Francisco, agrees; in an opinion piece that looks back at twenty years in IPE, two of the key issues he laments are the limited use of theory and the fact that in most places IPE is university based and has not extended sufficiently into the clinical areas.[1]

Although research into the impact of interprofessional care (IPC) on patient outcomes remains a conceptual conundrum, IPC is being celebrated for its ability to decrease tension and conflict among health care providers. "Satisfaction with the team that people work on is a huge predictor of why they stay with an organization," says Tassone. "On the team, people want to believe their voice is heard. People need to contribute beyond performing tasks. They want their ideas to be valued. They want opportunities to be a real part of the organization."

Today, U of T has embraced IPE and is ready to take it to the next level. "Interprofessional education as a mandated longitudinal curriculum was a great starting-point," says Verma, "but we still train in silos. There are small pockets of IPE electives and small pockets of IPE in the curriculum, but they're only add-ons. We need to map out the curriculum to see where there are redundancies. Health science students for the most part learn anatomy, physiology, pharmacology. They all learn ethics, they all learn professionalism, they all learn communication skills. So why are we teaching them separately?"

"Huge numbers of courses in the undergraduate medical program could be taught interprofessionally," says Rosenfield, a pediatrician. "In theory, there is very little that cannot be taught interprofessionally and very little that must be taught uniprofessionally." "In the health sciences, IPE will become our way of doing business," predicts Tassone. "The future is really about integrating IPE into schedules so we have common curriculum time and common curriculum content. We could really explode the curriculum."

CHALLENGES

Before IPE can explode across the campus, though, there are challenges to overcome. "The logistical problems of integrating IPE are significant," says Rosenfield. "They require a major shift in how we operate and a much more flexible structure." The biggest stumbling block, he says, will be integrating clinical placements. "The faculty are already stretched. You may want to sit and debrief with students, but you have thirty patients waiting to see you." Is the logistical angst surmountable? "Absolutely!" Rosenfield says. "These are just rigidities from the past."

Verma agrees: "The truth of the matter is that there is a very deep-seated fear of change. But it can all happen. If you have a good case, you can find a strategy and a solution. I do believe that everything has a solution."

An integrated curriculum will need to be supported by novel learning modalities, Verma continues. "We need to recognize that our students are technology driven and capable of

"From a student perspective, you have to know that your role matters, and that your skill set is important... knowing what other professionals do improved communication and improves patient care."

– Lisa Wu, Pharmacy student

learning a great deal through online courses. When students are sitting in a lecture hall, they're more engaged in social media than they are in listening to you or watching your PowerPoint."

Sioban Nelson is less convinced that shared content will lead to revolutionary change. She believes students segment back into their groups and tribes within integrated classes unless team-based training becomes a key focus of every class and is included in the assessment. The risk here, according to Nelson, would be of overexposure to IPE and student disengagement with the issue. For Nelson the big challenge is for IPE to evolve into a full-fledged team training curriculum that directly prepares learners for IPC. She would also like to see postlicensure education embraced to involve master of nursing students (e.g., nurse practitioners) and residents. "Building that continuum from early principles through to continuing education aligns with the hospitals' goals and gives our learners an amazing opportunity to evolve and mature as effective team members."

As IPE/C continues to build momentum across North America and beyond, a critical stumbling block remains the challenge of developing a strong partnership between practice and education. One of U of T's early innovators in IPE, Lynne Sinclair—who now consults with programs in the United States in her role as Innovative Program and External Development Lead at the Centre for IPE—emphasizes the need for a bilateral approach that engages education and practice. Sinclair tells the Centre's clients: "If you don't have your partners at the table, don't start. Go back and get your partners and then start." According to Sinclair, the big difference with Toronto was that "We intentionally partnered academia and practice from the very beginning of our IPE/IPC journey. Our American colleagues had been much earlier pioneers in the field; however, many of their initiatives and projects were not sustainable due to solo efforts of one sector and not the other. We knew that IPE and IPC were interdependent with each other, and thus it was a shared approach that would be truly transformative."

Sinclair has been part of the Toronto journey from the beginning, and for her the key lessons are to focus on partnerships and relationships. She cautions people not to get hung up on everything being "ready" or perfect—because it will never happen. "Find good partners and work with them," she advises, "all will follow from that." Susan Wagner, another

long-standing IPE pioneer and leader, agrees: "If we'd tried to make everything right, we never would have gotten anywhere." She adds, "You can start with a plan, but everything is constantly in flux. You have to roll with the punches! And look how far we've come!"

Not waiting till every duck is lined up, but not starting before you are ready may sound like contradictory messages. One key resource developed by a team from Toronto helps organizations figure out when to push the start button and guides them on how to get their organizations to that green light stage. Kathryn Parker, director of Academic Affairs at Holland Bloorview Kids Rehabilitation Hospital and evaluation advisor at the Centre for IPE, and Ivy Oandasan co-developed the Interprofessional Collaborative Organizational Map and Preparedness Assessment (IP-COMPASS). This very useful tool is a quality improvement instrument that assists organizations to determine their readiness for IPE/C. It consists of a fifteen-page workbook and self-assessment guide that allows organizations to rate and improve the readiness of clinical settings, in essence helping to surface how the organizational culture supports IPE/C.[2] By activating a team-based approach it allows for the pooling of expertise, knowledge, and perspectives factoring input from clinicians, leaders, and learners. It also allows for IPE/C to be embedded within an organization's broader quality framework and has direct relevance for organization and educational program accreditation.

What has been remarkable about the IP-COMPASS project, shares Parker, is how it has been taken up and used by the field in ways they never anticipated. IP-COMPASS began its life as a tool to assess organizational readiness for IPE/C. From the start, Parker and Oandasan were advised by participants to expand it to include a component that assisted with capacity building. Since that time it has been used by organizations as part of their quality frameworks and strategic planning. Parker has been surprised and delighted by the demand for the tool. "What we are learning is that organizations really benefit from the opportunity to create a structured conversation about assessing and optimizing team functioning."

The approach establishes an internal team that is then tasked to begin the discussion about teamwork that can potentially engage the whole organization. It is a facilitated guided organizational self-assessment around where the organization sits regarding IPE/C. The result is powerful. Just having the structured conversation is an intervention in itself. What is even more exciting is that the IP-COMPASS tool allows for the emergence of a common language *between* organizations. So once an organization has undergone the self-assessment, they might de-

cide they need to develop more coaching and support for IPE/C facilitators and create a mentorship program, for example. Because of IP-COMPASS they can communicate precisely what they are looking for to another organization and adopt their mentorship program rather than having to start from scratch and spend the resources on developing their own. The ability of this tool to foster collaboration and partnership has been one of the most exciting outcomes for Parker. "What we have found is that it is all about liberating processes to take an organization to another level. That way, the system gets smarter and we all do better. It's incredibly exciting work."[3]

The issue of organizational readiness and engagement of all practice constituencies continues to be the subject of research from the Toronto group. Published in *Academic Medicine* in 2012, Lingard, now at Western University, Ontario and director of the Centre for Education Research and Innovation (CERI), and colleagues directly tackle one of the big issues in interprofessional education —leadership, specifically physician leadership.[4] The article raises important questions concerning the wide gap between the self-perception of physicians as collaborative versus the perceptions of other team members. It also brings to the fore the complexities involved in shifting from hierarchical to collective forms of clinical practice and the inherent challenges to physicians who have been educated and mentored to see themselves as the natural leaders of patient care teams. As Oandasan puts it, "You have to be open to dismantling the structures that exist because they don't necessarily support interprofessional education or practice."

Even more challenging, though, are the related broad system issues that bedevil health care professional practice. For example, there continue to be structural disincentives to team practice that arise from regulation concerning professional practice and legal liability. The fundamental question that is answered differently by lawyers both across and within jurisdictions concerns which health professionals bear which accountabilities, and, in the case of problems, who is liable. Shared liability is a complex issue. Among physicians there remains a perception, whether justified or not, that most systems continue to require identification of a "most responsible physician" (MRP) who bears a major, and perhaps a disproportionate degree of responsibility for patient outcomes. But is the MD always the accountable individual on a team? Uncertainty about this crucial issue can raise questions concerning willingness to participate in shared decision making and anxieties about perceived risks for physician members of teams.

https://www.
mededportal.org/
publication/9257

Further, accreditation standards for service providers have not yet created the expectation that quality care must be pro-

vided in a multiprofessional or inter-professional way. What then are the institutional drivers to build physician engagement given the reasons cited above? For the health professional education programs the expectations of accreditors and regulators are changing, with some already requiring a high level of interprofessional education, such as pharmacy, while others are less clear, such as nursing; for medicine, the requirement is coming down the pike.

> "Ultimately the effectiveness that comes out of having good teamwork and mutual respect in tandem with open leadership and communication is what creates efficiency."
>
> – Navjot Raj, Medicine, IPHSA

Finally, the big issue that works against teamwork becoming the centerpiece of health care is *funding*. How do the funding models and payment systems reinforce the status quo and actively work against redesigning care to be a team sport?

Fee-for-service, the health service payment model that ties funding to specific activities, tops a long list, where payment incentivizes a physician-centric model of care. This payment model gives no incentive to physicians to spend time on activities that are not remunerated. But it is more complex than that. Entire institutions are funded for services and staffed accordingly on uniprofessional streams. Further, in Canada, physicians, medical residents, and fellows are not paid from hospital budgets so there can be reluctance to shift tasks to other health professionals, when doing so increases hospitals' direct costs. Untangling the way dollars flow to services and to health professionals is paramount to changing the basis of care to meet patient and community needs.

These abiding system issues have deep effects and can be expressed in the reluctance of particular team members to engage in IPE—if they don't see it as a viable practice model then they will not put time and energy into learners. While the Institute of Medicine (IOM), Health Canada, and WHO are calling for total change to a new and more sustainable model of health human resources and care delivery, the factors that hold the current system in place must be dislodged, or at least loosened, for sustained and generalized change to take place.

One of the global initiatives to facilitate that change is an IOM Board on Global Health–sponsored project that was named as one of four Innovation Collaboratives around the world to be incubators for new ideas that globally transform education and health. Four Collaboratives were selected through a peer-review process based on proposed projects that would leverage the recommendations from the Lancet

"Time and improved coordinated care were lost when my therapies were independent of one another. I know this because when I did find a collaborative team of interprofessional care providers, I, and my family, observed how my recovery improved dramatically as well as my morale."

– Health Mentor Program Mentor

Commission report on the "Education of Health Professionals for the 21st Century."[5] The U of T, with Maria Tassone and Sarita Verma as co-leads, heads up the only North American Collaborative: a national consortium of five universities known as the Canadian Interprofessional Health Leadership Collaborative (CIHLC). The group is developing a collaborative leadership program targeted to senior health care leaders. It will define and confer the collaborative leadership competencies required to lead health systems transformation and socially accountable change in order to confront complex health challenges. It is also working with the other three innovation collaboratives in South Africa, India, and Uganda to develop and disseminate the lessons learned from these different projects. As Verma puts it, "Leadership is about dealing with uncertainty, having a vision, having courage, and refusing to be a victim of circumstances. That's why this work developing global leaders across health care systems is so exciting!"

Achieving the end goal of system change for collaborative care and new models of practice will require more than new approaches to pedagogy. If one looks to the airline industry there are parallels and lessons to be learned. Aviation suffered a loss of public confidence with a series of catastrophic preventable crashes in the late 1970s and early 1980s. Eventually regulators, policymakers, insurers, and the public demanded its transformation from a risky to a safe industry. The success of the airline industry to reinvent itself from a high to a low risk industry relied upon a new model of practice and its center piece was the team. The development and implementation of Crew Resource Management (CRM) in the aviation industry involved an intensive and sustained program of training as well as commitment from leadership, regulators, unions, and government. As Suzanne Gordon and co-authors point out in *Beyond the Checklist: What Else Health Care Can Learn from Aviation Teamwork and Safety*,[6] the aviation industry had to initiate change at a systemwide level well before the results of this experiment in industry re-engineering were clear to anyone. People had to believe it was important to change and that it would work. Gordon dedicates a chapter of her book to the U of T Centre for IPE as a case study of how

http://cihlc.ca

health care and education culture *is* shifting to one that is more collaborative, team-oriented, and, ultimately, positioned to improve patient safety. But to fully shift health care from a practice that is provider-centric, poorly integrated, and with unacceptably high error rates will require the same kind of determination and comprehensive approach undertaken in the aviation industry. For IPE to confound the critics and be more than a fad, it needs to evolve into a mechanism to create the change and build the future of health care.

Educators simply can't wait for the system to be ready. To prepare the next generation of health professionals to be comfortable—and even to prefer—to work collaboratively in teams will take decades. The goal is that the new generation will not be the same as their teachers. As health professionals who see themselves first and foremost as team members they will make the change the system needs to provide better care.

15 Accreditation for education programs and service providers

16 Evaluation—new directions

17 Competency in interprofessional education and practice

CHAPTER 5

Reflection Questions: Thinking about Impact and Sustainability from the Start

These reflection questions are to focus on the future. A vision for success that is sustainable and long term is fundamental for building a new way of practice and new systems of care.

1. What is happening in the health education and care systems, locally, regionally, nationally, and internationally, that you will need to pay attention to as we build and grow an IPE/C program?

2. What will success of your IPE/C program look like ... in the short and longer term? What are the milestones along the way?

3. Who will need to be involved in order to achieve success?

4. How will you create and sustain momentum and enthusiasm as you go forward?

5. What are the critical evaluation, assessment, and research questions you will ask to understand your impact? What do your various stakeholders value?

6. How will you influence the necessary shifts in accreditation, regulation, and policy needed to fully enable IPE/C?

Notes

INTRODUCTION

1 Institute of Medicine, *To Err Is Human: Building a Safer Health System*, ed. L.T. Kohn, J.M. Corrigan, and M.S. Donaldson (Washington, D.C.: National Academy Press, 1999).

2 World Health Organization, *Framework for Action on Interprofessional Education and Collaborative Practice* (Geneva: WHO, 2010), accessed 1 April 2013, http://www.who.int/hrh/resources/framework_action/en.

3 J. Frenk, L. Chen, Z. Bhutta, J. Cohen, N. Crips, T. Evans, et al., Health professionals for a new century: transforming education to strengthen health systems in an interdependent world, *The Lancet* 376 (2010): 1923–1958, accessed 1 April 2013, doi:10.1016/S0140-6736(10)61854-5.

4 S. Gordon, P. Mendenhall, and B.B. O'Connor, *Beyond the Checklist, What Else Health Care Can Learn from Aviation Teamwork and Safety* (Ithaca: Cornell University Press, 2012).

5 "Proposed Accreditation Standard ED-19-A," *Liaison Committee on Public Education.* http://www.lcme.org/new_standard_ed-19-a.htm.

6 *"World Health Organization (2010): Framework for Action on Interprofessional Education & Collaborative Practice," (Geneva: WHO, 2010), access 1 April 2013, http://whqlibdoc.who.int/hq/2010/WHO_HRH_HPN_10.3_eng.pdf.*

7 Closson, T., and I. Oandasan, I. (July 2007). *Interprofessional Care: Blueprint for Action in Ontario.* Toronto, ON: Ministry of Health and Long-Term Care, http://www.healthforceontario.ca/UserFiles/file/PolicymakersResearchers/ipc-blueprint-july-2007-en.pdf.

CHAPTER 1

1 Martin L. Friedland, *The University of Toronto: A History,* 2nd ed. (Toronto: University of Toronto Press, 2013), x–xi.

2 Ibid.

3 Institute of Medicine, *To Err Is Human: Building a Safer Health System*, ed. L.T. Kohn, J.M. Corrigan, and M.S. Donaldson (Washington, D.C.: National Academy Press, 1999).

4   Commission on the Future of Health Care in Canada, *Building on Values: The Future of Health Care in Canada—Final Report*, ed. R. Romanow (Saskatoon, CA: Government of Canada Publications, November 2002) (CP32-85/2002E-IN).

5   I. Oandasan, et al., *Teamwork in Healthcare: Promoting Effective Teamwork in Healthcare in Canada: Policy Synthesis and Recommendations* (Ottawa, ON: Canadian Health Services Research Foundation, 2006), http://www.cfhi-fcass.ca/Migrated/PDF/ResearchReports/CommissionedResearch/teamwork-synthesis-report_e.pdf.

6   "Interprofessional Care: A Blueprint for Action in Ontario." Source: http://www.healthforceontario.ca/UserFiles/file/PolicymakersResearchers/ipc-blueprint-july-2007-en.pdf.

7   Healthforce Ontario, *Implementing Interprofessional Care in Ontario—Final Report of the Interprofessional Care Strategic Implementation Committee*, accessed 1 April 2013, http://www.healthforceontario.ca/UserFiles/file/PolicymakersResearchers/ipc-final-report-may-2010-en.pdf.

8   L. Lingard, S. Espin, S. Whyte, G. Regehr, G. R. Baker, R. Reznick et al., Communication failures in the operating room: An observational classification of recurrent types and effects, *Quality and Safety in Health Care* 13, no. 5 (2004): 330–34, doi:10.1136/qhc.13.5.330.

9   L. Lingard, G. Regehr, B. Order, R. Reznick, G. R. Baker, D. Doran et al., Evaluation of a preoperative checklist and team briefing among surgeons, nurses and anesthesiologist to reduce failures in communication, *Archives of Surgery* 143, no. 1 (2008): 12–17. Discussion 18. doi:10.1001/archsung.2007.21.

10   For example, a $3.4 million IMPLC—Catalyzing and Sustaining Communities of Collaboration around Interprofessional Care (CCIC) project was funded by the Ministry of Health and Long-Term Care (MOHLTC) in 2007. The project was a collaborative partnership between the University of Toronto and the Toronto Academic Health Sciences Network (TAHSN) that enabled TAHSN teaching hospitals to become active interprofessional care learning laboratories for future generations of health care providers.

CHAPTER 2

1   A.N. Haynes, T.G. Weiser, W.R. Berry, S.R. Lipsitz, A.H. Breizat, E.P. Dellinger et al., A surgical safety checklist to reduce morbidity and mortality in a global population, *New England Journal of Medicine* 360, no. 5 (2009): 491–9. doi:10-1056/NEJMsa0810119.

2   M. Marr, K. Hemmert, A. H. Nguyen, R. Combs, A. Annamalai, G. Miller et al., Team play in surgical education: A simulation-based study, *Journal of Surgical Education* 69, no. 1 (2012): 63–69.

3   L.M. Stevens, J.B. Cooper, D.B. Raemer, R.C. Schneider, A.S. Frankel, W.R. Berry, and A.K. Agnihotri, Educational program in crisis management for cardiac surgery teams including high realism simulation, *Journal of Thoracic and Cardiovascular Surgery* 144, no. 1 (2012): 17–24.

4   A. Bleakley, J. Allard, A. Hobbs, Towards culture change in the operating theatre: Embedding a complex educational intervention to improve teamwork climate, *Medical Teacher* 34 (2012): e635–e640.

CHAPTER 3

1   G. Charles, L. Bainbridge, and J. Gilbert, The University of British Columbia model of interprofessional education, *Journal of Interprofessional Care* 24, no. 1 (Jan. 2010): 9–18, doi:10.3109/ 13561820903294549.

2   Institute of Medicine of the National Academies, *Preventing Medication Errors*, (Washington, D.C.: National Academies Press, 2007), 124.

CHAPTER 4

1   "Interprofessional Mentoring Preceptorship Leadership and Coaching Super Toolkit," Centre for Interprofessional Education, University of Toronto, http://www.ipe.utoronto.ca/initiatives/ipc/implc/supertoolkit.html.

2   "Enhancing Interprofessional Practice: A Resource Manual for Team Coaches," St. Joseph's Health Centre (Toronto), http://www.stjoe.on.ca/education/pdf/Enhancing%20IP%20Practice%20Resource%20Manual%20-%20Part%201%20of%203.pdf.

CHAPTER 5

1   S. Reeves, Interprofessional education—Reflecting upon the past, scanning the future, The Josiah Macy Jr. Foundation, News and Commentary, accessed 1 April 2013, http://macyfoundation.org/news/entry/interprofessional-education-scott-reeves.

2   K. Parker, M. McGuire, I. Oandasan, R. Zorzi, "The Interprofessional Collaborative Organization Map and Preparedness Assessment Tool (IP-COMPASS)," MedEdPORTAL, 2012, Available from:www.mededportal.org/publication/9257.

3   K. Parker, A. Jacobson, M. McGuire, R. Zorzi, I. Oandason, How to build high-quality interprofessional collaboration and education in your hospital: The IP-COMPASS tool, *Quality Management in Health Care* 21, no. 3 (2012): 160–8.

4   L. Lingard, M. Vanstone, M. Durrant, B. Fleming-Carroll, M. Lowe, J. Rashotte, L. Sinclari, S. Tallett, Conflicting messages: Examining the dynamics of leadership on interprofessional teams, *Academic Medicine* 87, no. 12 (2012):1762–7.

5   A. Zulfiqar, L. Bhutta, J. Chen, N. Cohen, T. Crisp, H. Evans, et al., Education of health professionals for the 21st century: a global independent Commission, *The Lancet* 375, no. 9721 (3 April 2010): 1137-1138, doi:10.1016/S0140-6736(10)60450-3.

6   S. Gordon, P. Mendenhall, B. Blair O'Connor, *Beyond the Checklist: What Else Health Care Can Learn from Aviation Teamwork and Safety* (Ithaca, NY: Cornell University Press, 2013).

Further Reading

SELECT TORONTO SCHOLARSHIP ON IPE/C[1]

THIS WORKBOOK HAS FOCUSED ON THE REAL-LIFE CHALLENGES FACING EDUCATORS TRYing to advance their curricula and programs on the interprofessional education and care (IPE/C) front. Throughout the book, we provide multiple strategies and tactics to tackle these challenges. Supporting this practical advice is a wealth of scholarship generated by faculty across the Toronto Academic Health Science Centre. Over the years, faculty have successfully obtained funding for IPE/C initiatives, conducted evaluations, and written papers and reports that were widely disseminated. In this Further Reading section we provide an annotated bibliography on the scholarship produced at University of Toronto that built the Toronto IPE/C Model.

Abramovich, I., Espin, S., Wickson-Griffiths, A., Dematteo, D., Baker, L., Egan-Lee, E., & Reeves, S. (2011). Translating collaborative knowledge into practice: Findings from a 6-month follow-up study. *Journal of Interprofessional Care*, 25(3), 226–7.

A qualitative case study approach was used to evaluate the effect of an interprofessional graduate elective course for nursing and nutrition students. Two sets of interviews were conducted, one after the course's completion and one six months later, to explore whether the course had an effect on participants' approaches to collaborative work. Initial impact findings suggest a gain of knowledge and confidence, in aspects of collaboration with other professionals, and long-term findings report a sustained outlook of knowledge.

Akeroyd, J., Oandasan, I., Alsaffar, A., Whitehead, C., & Lingard, L. (2009). Perceptions of the Registered Nurse role in interprofessional primary care: Role and awareness and trustworthiness in collaborative practice. *Canadian Journal of Nursing Leadership*, 22(2), 73–84.

The authors describe health professionals' perceptions regarding registered nurse (RN) practice in

---

[1]This annotated bibliography includes only papers where the first or second author is a University of Toronto faculty member or student. It is also limited to reports and articles published between 2005 and 2013.

primary care. Qualitative data was collected from twenty-three providers working in three interprofessional academic family practice units. Findings suggest that there is ambiguity regarding the RN role in family practice, particularly in interprofessional settings. Recommendations include further examination of role clarity, as well as the impact of trust in developing collaborative environments.

Atack, L., Parker, K., Rocchi, M., Maher, J., & Dryden, T. (2009). The impact of an online interprofessional course in disaster management competency and attitude towards interprofessional learning. *Journal of Interprofessional Care, 23*(6): 586–98.

The authors assess the impact of an interprofessional interactive course developed to educate students across five faculties on the basics of disaster management. The course was found to be effective in providing an introduction to disaster management as well as in increasing the students' appreciation and awareness of interprofessional team members.

Austin, Z., Gregory, P.A., & Martin, J.C. (2007). Negotiation of interprofessional culture shock: The experience of pharmacists who become physicians. *Journal of Interprofessional Care, 21*(1), 83–93.

This qualitative study explores the experiences of pharmacists who have become physicians. Results highlight four major themes that depict salient and unique charac-

teristics of the cultures of medicine and pharmacy.

Bajcar, J.M., Kennie, N., & Einarson, T.R. (2005). Collaborative medication management in a team-based primary care practice: An exploratory conceptual framework. *Research in Social and Administrative Pharmacy, 1*(3), 408–29.

This article describes a conceptual framework to help identify, define, and discuss roles and responsibilities in collaborative medication management. The authors describe the framework in detail and discuss its value in the context of primary care roles.

Baker, L., Egan-Lee, E., Leslie, K., Silver, I., & Reeves, S. (2010). Exploring an IPE faculty development program using the 3–P model. *Journal of Interprofessional Care, 24*(5), 597–600.

The authors describe the results of a longitudinal systems-based evaluation of a faculty development program created to support IPE facilitators. A single case study design was utilized to explore the interaction of aspects related to the development, implementation, and outcomes of the new program.

Baker, L., Egan-Lee, E., Martimianakis, M.A., & Reeves, S. (2011). Relationships of power: Implications for interprofessional education. *Journal of Interprofessional Care, 25*(2), 98–104.

Using Witz's model of professional closure, the authors explore

the unequal power relations that exist between health and social care professions. Interviews with twenty-five health providers illuminate how different professionals' beliefs regarding interprofessional interactions and behaviours either reinforce or restructure traditional power relationships.

Baker, L., Reeves, S., Egan-Lee, E., Leslie, K., & Silver, I. (2010). The ties that bind: Network approach to creating a programme in faculty development. *Medical Education, 44*(2), 132–9.

This discussion paper proposes the use of a "fishhook" model of faculty development program formation. The proposed model is based on seven key factors that are tenets of network theory. The overall aim is to support medical educators to teach contemporary topics, including IPE and social accountability.

Baker, T.L., Boyce, J., Gairy, P., & Mighty, G. (2011). Interprofessional management of a complex continuing care patient admitted with 18 pressure ulcers: A case report. *Ostomy Wound Management, 57*(2), 38–47.

The authors describe a case report regarding a 44-year-old man with significant skin breakdown. The article highlights how the use of interprofessional team management strategies facilitated the care and healing of the patient's wounds. Interprofessional collaboration is hailed as an important approach to managing complex continuing care patients.

Barker, K.K., & Oandasan, I. (2005). Interprofessional care review with medical residents: Lessons learned, tensions aired—A pilot study. *Journal of Interprofessional Care, 19*(3), 207–14.

An interprofessional care education initiative for medical residents was evaluated using one-on-one interviews and a focus group for initiative participants. The results indicated that residents valued the initiative, but felt that "mixed messages" were given by supervisors in regard to the benefit of collaborating with other health professionals.

Boaro, N., Fancott, C., Baker, R., Velji, K., & Andreoli, A. (2010). Using SBAR to improve communication in interprofessional rehabilitation teams. *Journal of Interprofessional Care, 24*(1), 111–4.

This study evaluates the SBAR communication tool in a rehabilitation setting as opposed to the acute setting where the tool is commonly used. The SBAR tool was implemented in an interprofessional rehabilitation clinic for six months, and focus groups as well as interviews with patients, family members, and staff were used to assess the tool's impact. The results showed the SBAR tool's capabilities to improve communication in a nonurgent setting.

Bogo, M., Paterson, J., Tufford, L., & King, R. (2011). Supporting front-

line practitioners' professional development and job satisfaction in mental health and addiction. *Journal of Interprofessional Care, 25*(3), 209–14.

This exploratory study examines practitioners' perceptions of their professional work. Focus groups were conducted with seventy-six practitioners, representing six different professions, from a large urban mental health facility. The authors identify three interrelated factors that influence practitioners' perceptions about their competence and job satisfaction:

(1) supervision from experts;
(2) collaborative, interprofessional teams; and
(3) organizational support. The value of stable, cohesive teams on provider perceptions is discussed as it relates to turnover and organizational performance.

Boon, H.S., Mior, S.A., Barnsley, J., Ashbury, F.D., & Haig, R. (2009). The difference between integration and collaboration in patient care: Results from key informant interviews working in multiprofessional health care teams. *Journal of Manipulative and Physiological Therapeutics, 32*(9), 715–22.

This qualitative study explores how practitioners perceive and define the terms *integration* and *collaboration* in the patient care context. Semi-structured interviews were conducted with sixteen key informants. Results from the qualitative content analysis suggest that integration requires collaboration as a precondition, but collaboration does not require integration.

Cameron, A., Ignjatovic, M., Langlois, S., Dematteo, D., DiProspero, L., Wagner, S., & Reeves, S. (2009). An interprofessional education session for first-year health science students. *American Journal of Pharmaceutical Education, 73*(4), 62.

This study evaluates the effectiveness and the short-term impact of an interprofessional session conducted in the first year of studies across nine health care disciplines at the University of Toronto. The results indicate that the session served as an effective introduction to IPE but that an interest exists for additional small group interactions as well as session debriefings.

Cameron, A., Ignjatovic, M., Langlois, S., Dematteo, D., DiProspero, L., Wagner, S., & Reeves, S. (2010). An introduction to teamwork: Findings from an evaluation of an interprofessional education experience for 1,000 first-year health science students. *Journal of Allied Health, 38*(4), 220–6.

A mixed-method pre/post research design was utilized to track the changes in students' outlooks and attitudes regarding IPE after they participated in a large-scale first year IPE session. In total, 399 surveys were matched for pre/post analysis; in addition, twenty-five students also participated in focus group interviews. Results indicate that despite logistical challenges, it is feasible to offer a successful IPE

session to a large group of first-year students.

Carr, E., & Watt-Watson, J. (2012). Interprofessional pain education: Definitions, exemplars and future directions. *British Journal of Pain*, 6(2), 59–65.

The authors argue that educational preparation for health care practitioners should include interprofessional learning opportunities to help prepare them for the successful management of pain, which often requires interprofessional care. Survey data suggests that the curriculum of most health care professionals does not provide them with interprofessional learning opportunities surrounding pain management. Harnessing the political agenda is suggested for the implementation of additional pain education programs for health care practitioners.

Cheung, D., McKellar, J., Parsons, J., Lowe, M., Willems, J., Heus, L., & Reeves, S. (2012). Community re-engagement and interprofessional education: The impact on health care providers and persons living with stroke. *Topics in Stroke Rehabilitation*, 19(1), 63–74.

A mixed-methods study was conducted to evaluate the impact of an educational intervention on health care providers' practice with stroke patients. The intervention integrates concepts of community re-engagement and interprofessional collaboration. The

authors found significant increases in positive perceptions of care and practice.

Closson, T., & Oandasan, I. (July 2007). *Interprofessional care: Blueprint for action in Ontario*. Toronto, ON: Ministry of Health and Long-Term Care, http://www.healthforceontario.ca/UserFiles/file/PolicymakersResearchers/ipc-blueprint-july-2007-en.pdf.

This report, put forward by the Ministry of Health and Long-Term Care's Interprofessional Care Steering Committee, outlines a blueprint to guide Ontario's strategy regarding interprofessional care. It captures input from a wide range of stakeholders and provides a framework for health care organizations, educational institutions, and regulatory bodies to utilize when moving interprofessional care forward.

Conn, L.G., Lingard, L., Reeves, S., Miller, K.L., Russell, A., & Zwarenstein, M. (2009). Communication channels in general internal medicine: A description of baseline patterns for improved interprofessional collaboration. *Qualitative Health Research*, 19(7), 943–53.

This article comments on an ethnographic study of health professionals' communication conducted in two general internal medicine wards using the lens of genre theory. Findings reveal a significant relationship between synchronous and asynchronous modes of communication. The

implications are discussed as well as ideas to help overcome existing interprofessional communication barriers.

D'Amour, D., & Oandasan, I. (2005). Interprofessionality and interprofessional education for collaborative patient-centred practice: An evolving framework. *Journal of Interprofessional Care, 19*(Suppl. 1), 8–20.

This seminal paper defines, and makes the case for, the use of the concept *interprofessionality*. Here, interprofessionality is concerned with the processes and determinants that influence IPE initiatives, as well as interprofessional collaboration. The authors also use this concept as the basis for a framework that bridges the gap between interprofessional education and interprofessional practice (at the micro, meso, and macro levels).

Dematteo, D., & Reeves, S. (2011). A critical examination of the role of appreciative inquiry within an interprofessional health care initiative. *Journal of Interprofessional Care, 25*(3), 203–8.

Fifty interviews gathered from a wider study of IPE are analyzed using a multiple case study approach. The common themes that emerged offered an understanding of appreciative inquiry within this particular IPE initiative. Findings suggest that the use of appreciative inquiry can overlook many structural factors, which may hinder its ability to add significant and lasting change within the field of health care.

Dugani, S., & McGuire, R. (2011). Development of IMAGINE: A three-pillar student initiative to promote social accountability and interprofessional education. *Journal of Interprofessional Care, 25*(6), 454–6.

This short report discusses the IMAGINE initiative, a student run group that promotes social accountability and interprofessional education and care. The group offers a variety of educational lectures targeted toward marginalized groups in Toronto, as well as a Saturday interprofessional care clinic run by students and faculty preceptors.

Egan-Lee, E., Baker, L., Tobin, S., Hollenberg, E., Dematteo, D., & Reeves, S. (2011). Neophyte facilitator experiences of interprofessional education: Implications for faculty development. *Journal of Interprofessional Care, 25*(5), 333–8.

The authors draw data from a multiple case study of four IPE programs based in North America to evaluate the effectiveness of current training initiatives in place for IPE facilitators. Findings indicate that many facilitators still felt unprepared to lead their groups and had a poor conceptual understanding of core IP principles after having completed their training.

Egan-Lee, E., Hollenburg, E., Dematteo, D., Tobin, S., Oandasan, I., Beduz, M.A., ... Reeves, S. (2008). Catalyzing and sustaining communities of collaboration around interprofessional care: An evaluation of four educational programs. *Journal of Interprofessional Care, 22*(3), 317–19.

This paper covers the "Catalyzing and Sustaining Communities of Collaboration around Interprofessional Care" project, which involved the coordination of the health science disciplines at the University of Toronto as well as the thirteen affiliated teaching hospitals. The project's goal was to increase knowledge, awareness, and skills for interprofessional practice.

Fournier, C., & Reeves, S. (2012). Professional status and interprofessional collaboration: A view of massage therapy. *Journal of Interprofessional Care, 26*(1), 71–72.

The authors utilize an exploratory case-study approach to discover perceptions of the professionalization and status of massage therapists as well as the implications surrounding interprofessional collaboration. The data analysis indicated a lack of knowledge of massage therapy in terms of its scope, education, and regulation, an exclusion of massage therapists in collaborative settings, a notion of massage therapists being at the lower end of the health care provider hierarchy, and a problematization of the term *massage*.

Furness, S., Hyslop-St George, C., Pound, B., Earle, M., Maurich, A., Rice, D. &

Humpl, T. (2008). Development of an interprofessional pediatric ventricular assist device support team. *American Society for Artificial Internal Organs, 54*(5), 483–5.

The article describes the phases undertaken to create an interprofessional ventricular assist device team. The team was created in four phases: Initial Education, Core Team Formation, Expansion, and Evaluation. Due to the complex care required for a patient on a ventricular assist device, an interprofessional team helps ensure the best possible patient outcome.

Gallé, J., & Lingard, L. (2010). A medical student's perspective of participation in an interprofessional education placement: An autoethnography. *Journal of Interprofessional Care, 24*(6), 722–33.

This article presents an autoethnographic account of a medical student's IPE placement experience. The authors suggest incorporating reflexive activities within the IPE placements to help students develop a greater understanding of roles, responsibilities, and professional perspectives, as well as to enhance their critical thinking and professional growth.

Gardezi, F., Lingard, L., Espin, S., Whyte, S., Orser, B., & Baker, G.R. (2009). Silence, power and communication in the operating room. *Journal of Advanced Nursing, 65*(7), 1390–99.

This article examined the use of structured interprofessional team

briefing as a strategy to support communication in the operating room. The authors observed interprofessional communication throughout seven hundred surgical procedures and captured data using a critical ethnographic perspective. Results suggest that there are different forms of "silences" during team communication and they are related to power dynamics.

Gillan, C., Wiljer, D., Harnett, N., Briggs, K., & Catton, P. (2010). Changing stress while stressing change: The role of interprofessional education in mediating stress in the introduction of a transformative technology. *Journal of Interprofessional Care, 24*(6), 710–21.

This study aimed to explore the potential for an IPE approach to reduce the stress, and help with the facilitation, of the adoption of Image Guided Radiation Therapy. Fourteen interviews were conducted using a modified grounded theoretical approach. IPE was seen to benefit the implementation on transformative technologies by helping to mediate the stress associated with change.

Goldman, J. (2011). The contribution of ethnographic methods to our understanding of interprofessional teamwork. *Journal of Interprofessional Care, 25*(3), 165–6.

The author provides a commentary on a paper by A. Jones and D. Jones (2010) titled "Improving teamwork, trust and safety: An ethnographic study of an interprofessional initia-

tive." It provides insight regarding key conceptual and methodological issues and makes recommendations to help advance the field of interprofessional care.

Goldman, J., Meuser, J., Rogers, J., Lawrie, L., & Reeves, S. (2010). Interprofessional primary care protocols: A strategy to promote an evidence-based approach to teamwork and the delivery of care. *Journal of Interprofessional Care, 24*(6), 653–65.

A qualitative study is used to examine the process of pilot implementation and interprofessional protocol development. Thirty-six interviews were done with health professionals and community group members, along with the collection of observational and documentary data from the implementation processes. The implementation strategies used and the outcomes achieved are discussed.

Goldman, J., Meuser, J., Rogers, J., Lawrie, L., & Reeves, S. (2010). Interprofessional collaboration in family health teams: An Ontario-based study. *Canadian Family Physician, 56*(10), 368–74.

The study considers family health care team providers' perspectives and experiences regarding interprofessional collaboration. The health care team's perceived benefits of IPC are discussed and a framework is provided for understanding various types of IP interventions used to support IP collaborations.

Goldman, J., Zwarenstein, M., Bhattacharyya, O., & Reeves, S. (2009). Improving the clarity of the interprofessional field: Implications for research and continuing interprofessional education. *Journal of Continuing Education in the Health Professions, 29*(3), 151-6.

The authors report on research being undertaken to improve the interprofessional field's conceptual clarity and to identify aspects in need of further development. Emerging review findings are reported regarding interventions, participants, settings, and outcomes.

Gotlib Conn, L., Oandasan, I., Creede, C., Jakubovic, D., & Wilson, L. (2010). Creating sustainable change in the interprofessional academic primary care setting: An appreciative inquiry approach. *Journal of Research in Interprofessional Practice & Education, 1*(3), 284–300.

The authors report findings from the evaluation of an intervention to advance teamwork in an Ontario family health team. The intervention was developed using principles of Appreciative Inquiry. Findings revealed a change in team practice, such as patient-centredness and team discourse.

Hanna, E., Soren, B., Telner, D., Macneill, H., Lowe, M., & Reeves, S. (2013). Flying blind: The experience of online interprofessional facilitation. *Journal of Interprofessional Care, 27*(4), 298–304. doi:10.3109/13561820.2012.723071.

This report describes a qualitative study that sought to examine the experiences of facilitators using an online interprofessional course. Four major themes are discussed and the authors highlight that IPE facilitation was seen to carry over to the online setting.

Hoffman, S.J., Harris, A., & Rosenfield, D. (2008). Why mentorship matters: Students, staff and sustainability in interprofessional education. *Journal of Interprofessional Care, 22*(1), 103–5.

The authors discuss the merits of mentorship in the advancement of the interprofessional field and urge professionals to facilitate mentorship relationships with students to help shape the leaders of tomorrow.

Hoffman, S., Rosenfield, D., Gilbert, J., & Oandasan, I. (2008). Student leadership in interprofessional education: Benefits, challenges and implications for educators, researchers and policymakers. *Medical Education, 42*(7), 654–61.

The authors argue in support of the vital role that student leadership can play in facilitating the long-term sustainability of IPE efforts. A literature review was conducted and questionnaires administered to student leaders. The results showed tremendous potential for student-initiated IPE efforts as long as the support of educators, researchers, and policy makers continued to promote an environment conducive to student leadership opportunities.

Hoffman, S.J., Rosenfield, D., & Nasmith, L. (2009). What attracts students to interprofessional education and other health care reform initiatives? *Journal of Allied Health, 38*(3), 75–78.

This qualitative study examines the factors that attract students to IPE and other health care reform initiatives. Findings suggest that students tend to become involved in IPE initiatives after they joined a student organization or received encouragement from a teacher or peer. The authors discuss potential approaches to make IPE more attractive to students.

Hollenberg, E., Reeves, S., Beduz, M. A., Jeffs, L., Kwan, D., Lee, J., ... Oandasan, I. (2009). Mainstreaming interprofessional education within hospital settings: Findings from a multiple case study. *Journal of Research in Interprofessional Practice & Education, 1*(1),10-23.

A realistic evaluation framework was used to explore the impact of implementing a large, multi-site interprofessional education initiative in Ontario. Findings highlight how inter-organizational partnerships developed as a result of this project. As well, the researchers found a significant impact on individual, professional and organizational outcomes.

Jabbar, A. (2011). Language, power and implications for interprofessional collaboration: Reflections on a transition from social work to medicine. *Journal of Interprofessional Care, 25*(6), 447–8.

The author reflects on her experiences during her transition from social work to medicine. The manifestations of health care power dynamics are discussed in relation to the use of language and its implications for IPC. The author suggests that health care professions consider how language choice can be seen as a reflection of systemic power and that this discourse should be challenged in an attempt to develop a new shared language for IPC.

Karim, R., & Ross, C. (2008). Interprofessional education (IPE) and chiropractic. *Journal of the Canadian Chiropractic Association, 52*(2), 76–78.

Ross and Karim's commentary discusses the merits of interprofessional education across health-care disciplines. The authors propose a shift towards the inclusion of chiropractic colleges in inter-disciplinary health-care initiatives.

Kenaszchuk, C., Conn, L.G., Dainty, K., McCarthy, C., Reeves, S., & Zwarenstein, M. (2012). Consensus on interprofessional collaboration in hospitals: statistical agreement of ratings from ethnographic fieldwork and measurement scales. *Journal of Evaluation in Clinical Practice, 18*(1), 93-99.

Interprofessional collaboration was studied in seven hospitals using an ethnographer who shadowed and conducted interviews with regulated health care professionals. The hospitals were

ranked from 1-7 based on the interpretation of the field work. The fieldwork rankings were in line with contemporary IPC scales but less so with the Nursing Work Index.

Kenaszchuk, C., MacMillan, K., van Soeren, M., & Reeves, S. (2011). Interprofessional simulated learning: Short-term associations between simulation and interprofessional collaboration. *BioMed Central Medicine, 9, 29.*

This single-arm intervention study examined the association between measures of interprofessional collaboration and simulated team practice, as well as attitudes towards health care teams and nurse-physician relationships. The study results suggest that focusing interprofessional simulation education on shared leadership may help improve interprofessional care.

Kenaszchuk, C., Reeves, S., Nicholas, D., & Zwarenstein, M. (2010). Validity and reliability of a multiple-group measurement scale for interprofessional collaboration. *BMC Health Services Research, 10, 83.*

This article describes the development and testing of an interprofessional collaboration measurement scale suitable for multiple health provider groups. The tool was piloted with various providers from fifteen community and academic hospitals in Toronto. Certain elements were found to be valid and reliable; however, further testing is required.

Kitto, S., Chesters, J., Thistlethwaite, J., & Reeves, S., eds. *Sociology of Interprofessional Health Care Practice: Critical Reflections and Concrete Solutions.* **New York: Nova Science, 2011.**

This is an edited collection that examines interprofessional education from the perspective of critical sociology of the professions and health. With contributions from interdisciplinary scholars from Australia, Canada, and the United Kingdom, the book examines emerging issues in theory and practice, questions assumptions, and provides a reflective account of change and its challenges.

Kuper, A., & Whitehead, C. (2012). The paradox of interprofessional education: IPE as a mechanism of maintaining physician power. *Journal of Interprofessional Care. 26(5), 347–9.*

The benefits of interprofessional education are questioned as well as the rigor of existing studies conducted on the merits of IPE. The authors employ the lens of language to examine the social constructs surrounding IPE.

Kwan, D., Barker, K., Austin Z., Chatalalsingh, C., Grdisa V., Langlois S., ... Oandasan I. (2006). Effectiveness of a faculty development program on interprofessional education: A randomized controlled trial. *Journal of Interprofessional Care, 20(3), 314–16.*

This report provides an overview of a proposed randomized control trial study. The authors outline the anticipated methods and outcomes

of interest. See Kwan et al. (2009) for the published results.

Kwan, D., Barker, K., Richardson, D., Wagner, S.J., & Austin Z. (2009). Effectiveness of a faculty development program in fostering interprofessional education competencies. *Journal of Research in Interprofessional Practice and Education, 1*(1), 24–41.

This pre-post randomized control trial assessed the effectiveness of a faculty development program regarding IPE. No significant differences were noted between the control and intervention groups, as it relates to various outcome measures of faculty knowledge, skills, and attitudes in interprofessional care.

Lewin, S., & Reeves, S. (2011). Enacting "team" and "teamwork": Using Goffman's theory of impression management to illuminate interprofessional collaboration on hospital wards. *Social Science Medicine, 72*(10), 1595–1602.

Goffman's theory of impression management is used to explore how health care professionals "present" themselves during interaction on hospital wards as well as how they exhibit front stage and backstage settings during their collaborative work. The methods included forty-nine interviews of various health and social care staff as well as participant observation. The findings suggest that doctor–nurse relationships can be described as "parallel working," where limited information sharing or effective teamwork occurs.

Lineker, S.C., Bell, M.J., & Badley, E. (2011). Evaluation of an inter-professional educational intervention to improve the use of arthritis best practices in primary care. *Journal of Rheumatology, 38*(5), 931–7.

This paper describes an evaluation of a community-based, interprofessional continuing health education program, "Getting a Grip on Arthritis." Data from 553 primary care providers suggests that IPE may be an effective method for dissemination of best practice guides, as well as for improving patient care.

Lingard, L., Espin, S., Rubin, B., Whyte, M., Colmenares, G., Baker, R. ... Reznick, R. (2005). Getting teams to talk: Development and pilot implementation of a checklist to promote interprofessional communication in the OR. *Quality & Safety in Health Care, 14*(5), 340–6.

This article describes the pilot implementation of a preoperative team communication checklist. Results from field notes describe how the perceived functions of the checklist included a number of different aspects, including team building and decision making. The authors conclude that this checklist shows promise as a feasible and efficient tool that promotes information exchange and team cohesion.

Lingard, L., Gotlib Conn, L., Russell, A., Reeves, S., Miller, K.L., Kenaszchuk, C., & Zwarenstein, M. (2007). Interprofessional information work: Innovations in the use of the chart on internal medicine teams. *Journal of Interprofessional Care, 21*(6), 657–67.

This ethnographic study examines the nature and use of patient charts in two internal medicine inpatient wards. The authors provide an analysis of recurrent problems and adaptive strategies related to collaborative decision-making and care enactment with patient charts.

Lingard, L., Regehr, G., Espin, S., & Whyte, S. (2006). A theory-based instrument to evaluate team communication in the operating room: Balancing measurement authenticity and reliability. *Quality & Safety in Health Care, 15*(6), 422–6.

This prospective study assesses whether structured team briefing improves operating room communication. Results found that the use of a preoperative checklist reduced the number of communication failures between team members. The authors also discuss the value of interprofessional checklist briefings in promoting collaborative care.

Lingard, L., Regehr, G., Orser, B., Reznick, R., Baker, G.R., Doran, D. ... Whyte, S. (2008). Evaluation of a preoperative checklist and team briefing among surgeons, nurses and anesthesiologists to reduce failures in communication. *Archives of Surgery, 143*(1), 12–17.

This article is an extension of Lingard et al. (2005) and assesses whether structured team briefings improve operating room communication. One hundred and seventy-two procedures were observed in a Canadian academic tertiary care hospital. The authors found a significant reduction in the number of communication failures when using the interprofessional checklist.

Lingard, L., Whyte, S., Espin, S., Baker, G.R., Orser, B., & Doran, D. (2006). Towards safer interprofessional communication: Constructing a model of utility from preoperative team briefings. *Journal of Interprofessional Care, 20*(5), 471–83.

The authors analyze the discourse of structured preoperative team briefings by considering observers' field notes from 302 briefings. A two-part model of communicative "utility" emerged from the analysis. Ways in which altered communication patterns can help positively impact team awareness and behaviour are discussed.

Lumague, M., Morgan, A., Mak, D., Hanna, M., Kwong, J., Cameron, C. ... Sinclair, L. (2006). Interprofessional education: The student perspective. *Journal of Interprofessional Care, 20*(3), 246–53.

The authors discuss the benefits and challenges associated with an interprofessional clinical placement from the students' perspectives. Nine students from seven different faculties comment on

their five-week IP placement at the Toronto Rehabilitation Institute and generally respond positively about their experiences.

McKellar, J.M., Cheung, D., Lowe, M., Willems, J., Heus, L., & Parsons, J. (2011). Health-care providers' perspectives on an interprofessional education intervention for promoting community re-engagement post stroke. *Journal of Interprofessional Care, 25*(5), 380–2.

The authors evaluate an IPE intervention aimed to integrate IPC competencies into a community re-engagement framework. Participants reported an increased understanding of the competencies required for IPC as well as an improvement in their ability to work collaboratively in order to affect change in their approach to community re-engagement post-stroke.

Meffe, F., Moravac, C.C., & Espin, S. (2012). An interprofessional education pilot program in maternity care: Findings from an exploratory case study of undergraduate students. *Journal of Interprofessional Care, 26*(3), 183–8.

This study utilized an exploratory case study approach to assess whether participation in an IPE pilot program in maternity care would promote collaborative behaviour in the practice setting. Twenty-five semi-structured interviews were done during various time intervals up to twenty months after the program's completion date. Analysis of the

transcripts revealed four main themes: confident communication, willingness to collaborate, relationship building, and woman/family centered care.

Meuser, J., Bean, T., Goldman, J., & Reeves, S. (2006). Family health teams: A new Canadian interprofessional initiative. *Journal of Interprofessional Care, 20*(4), 436–8.

The authors describe the Ontario Ministry of Health and Long-Term Care's Family Health Team initiative. With the aid of the initiative, new family health care teams were emerging with few accessible IPE opportunities available. The development and evaluation of workshops created by the staff of the Centre for Effective Practice are discussed.

Miller, K.L., Reeves, S., Zwarenstein, M., Beales, J.D., Kenaszchuk, C., & Gotlib Conn, L. (2008). Nursing emotion work and interprofessional collaboration in general internal medicine wards: A qualitative study. *Journal of Advanced Nursing, 64*(4), 332–43.

This study examines nursing emotion in relation to interprofessional collaboration in an attempt to understand and improve collaborative nursing practice. Qualitative data was collected through nonparticipant observation, as well as shadowing and semi-structured interviews. Findings suggest that nurses' collaborations with other health professionals are impacted by emotion work considerations.

Moaveni A., Nasmith L., & Oandasan I. (2008). Building best practice in faculty development for inter-professional collaboration in primary care. *Journal of Interprofessional Care, 22*(Suppl. 1), 80–82.

This short report describes a project that examines how primary care educators can assist in advancing team-based practices. Results from focus groups highlight a number of barriers, needs, and solutions related to the development of collaborative practice in the clinical setting.

Oandasan, I. (2007). Teamwork and healthy workplaces: Strengthening the links for deliberation and action through research and policy. *Health Care Papers, 7*(Sp), 98–103.

The author provides a commentary on two lead articles written by Shamian and El-Jardali and by Clements, Dault, and Priest. Here, she outlines how the Ontario government has been engaging in a process to develop IPC as part of the healthy workplace agenda. Arguments are also made for enhancing teamwork in practice through targeted policy interventions.

Oandasan, I. (2009). The way we do things around here: Advancing an interprofessional care culture within primary care. *Canadian Family Physician, 55*(12), 1173–4.

This commentary speaks to possible strategies to help advance interprofessional practice in primary care. Current barriers are

discussed and recommendations presented regarding how to lead a shift in culture.

Oandasan, I., Baker, G.R., Barker, K., Bosco, C., D'Amour, D., Jones, L. ... Way, D. (2006). *Teamwork in healthcare: Promoting effective teamwork in healthcare in Canada. Policy Synthesis and recommendations.* Ottawa, ON: Canadian Health Services Research Foundation. http://www.cfhi-fcass.ca/Migrated/PDF/ResearchReports/CommissionedResearch/teamwork-synthesis-report_e.pdf.

This report provides a comprehensive policy synthesis of evidence regarding teamwork in health care. A number of different elements are addressed, including: the characteristics of an effective team, successful interventions that promote teamwork, current approaches being utilized in Canada and abroad, and challenges when sustaining efforts. Recommendations are made for the practice, organizational, and policy levels.

Oandasan, I., Gotlib Conn, L., Lingard, L., Karim, A., Jakubovicz, D., Whitehead C., ... Reeves S. (2009). The impact of time and space on interprofessional teamwork in Canadian primary care settings—Implications for health care reform. *Primary Health Care Research and Development, 10*(2), 151–62.

Using an ethnographic approach, the authors explored the nature of interprofessional teamwork in three family health centers. Findings suggest that the physical

layout and temporal organization of clinical practice leads to different approaches, and varying levels of success, with interprofessional teamwork.

Oandasan I., & Reeves, S. (2005). Key elements of interprofessional education: Part I. *Journal of Interprofessional Care, 19*(Suppl. 1), 21–38.

The first of two papers, this article discusses the learning context for IPE and considers questions related to the "who, what, where, when, and how." Informed by a systematic literature review, the authors provide a historical review of efforts in IPE, including pedagogical approaches and considerations of the learning context.

Oandasan I., & Reeves S. (2005). Key elements of interprofessional education: Part II. *Journal of Interprofessional Care, 19*(Suppl. 1), 39–48.

The second of two papers, this article considers factors for success in interprofessional education. Individual (micro), institutional (meso), and political (macro) factors are examined. Various outcome measures are discussed.

Paradis, E., & Reeves, S. (2013). Key trends in interprofessional research: A macrosociological analysis from 1970 to 2010. *Journal of Interprofessional Care, 27*(2), 113.

A macrosociological approach, along with a Bourdieusian theoretical framework, is used to examine the growth of the interprofessional research field since the 1970s. The articles are coded and analyzed both thematically and longitudinally. The results indicate a growing legitimacy of the field of interprofessional research.

Parker, K., Jacobson, A., McGuire, M., Zorzi, R., & Oandasan, I. (2012). How to build high-quality interprofessional collaboration and education in your hospital: The IP-COMPASS tool. *Quality Management in Health Care, 21*(3), 160–8.

This article describes the development and testing of a quality improvement framework, the Interprofessional Collaborative Organizational Map and Preparedness Assessment (IP-COMPASS). The authors discuss the importance of organizational culture in fostering environments that are conducive to interprofessional learning.

Pauzé, E., & Reeves, S. (2010). Examining the effects of interprofessional education on mental health providers: Findings from an updated systematic review. *Journal of Mental Health, 19*(3), 258–71.

The authors provide an updated systemic review of the effects of IPE on mental health professionals providing adult mental health care from 1967 to 1998. A triangulation approach was utilized to determine the quality of the evidence documented by the studies. The review notes an improvement in the methodological rigor of future research designs may be necessary.

Reeves, S. (2009). An overview of continuing interprofessional education. *Journal of Continuing Education in the Health Professions, 29*(3), 142–6.

This overview considers ten articles that provide a comprehensive overview of continuing interprofessional education. Reeves situates the ten articles within the seven key interprofessional trends that have emerged in the field.

Reeves, S., & Freeth, D. (2006). Re-examining the evaluation of interprofessional education for community mental health teams with a different lens: Understanding presage, process and product factors. *Journal of Psychiatric and Mental Health Nursing, 13*(6), 765–70.

This article examines the formative evaluation of a UK-based pilot project and tests the usefulness of a new framework for analysis. The authors argue that the presage-process-product (3P) framework should be utilized in the development of in-service IPE sessions.

Reeves, S., Freeth, D., Glen, S., Leiba, T., Berridge, E.J., & Herzberg, J. (2006). Delivering practice-based interprofessional education to community mental health teams: Understanding some key lessons. *Nurse Education in Practice, 6*(5), 246–53.

This paper describes an IPE initiative that was offered to two community mental health teams. A multi-method research design was utilized to collect data at four points in time. Results were positive and showed a general appreciation of the initiative as well as an enhanced understanding of collaboration.

Reeves, S., Goldman, J., Gilbert, J., Tepper, J., Silver, I., Suter, E., & Zwarenstein, M. (2011). A scoping review to improve conceptual clarity of interprofessional interventions. *Journal of Interprofessional Care, 25*(3), 167–74.

This article summarizes results from a scoping review of the interprofessional field. A total of 104 studies were included, and, through analysis of the data, an interprofessional framework was developed and tested. The final framework is comprised of three main categories of intervention (education, practice, and organization), while the outcomes are delineated as intermediate, patient, and system. The authors did not incorporate theoretical aspects into the framework because use of theory in the included studies was limited.

Reeves, S., Goldman, J., & Oandasan, I. (2007). Key factors in planning and implementing interprofessional education in health care settings. *Journal of Allied Health, 36*(4), 231–5.

The authors provide a commentary on key concepts that underpin IPE. They argue that seven interconnecting learner-focused, faculty-focused, and organization-focused factors are necessary

for the successful planning and implementation of IPE.

Reeves, S., Goldman, J., & Zwarenstein, M. (2009). An emerging framework for understanding the nature of interprofessional interventions. *Journal of Interprofessional Care*, 23(5), 539–42.

The authors conduct a scoping review of existing interprofessional literature in order to map out the key concepts, theories, sources of evidence, and gaps. An interprofessional collaboration framework emerges from the review.

Reeves, S., & Hean, S. (2013). Why we need theory to help us better understand the nature of interprofessional education, practice and care. *Journal of Interprofessional Care*, 27(1), 1–3.

This editorial focuses on the need for using theories (grand, midrange, and micro) to advance the field of interprofessional care, practice, and education. The authors identify the need for further use of sociological perspectives to enhance our understanding of how power imbalances and gender and ethnic differences are enacted in interprofessional care scenarios.

Reeves, S., Nelson, S., & Zwarenstein, M. (2008). The doctor–nurse game in the age of interprofessional care: A view from Canada. *Nursing Inquiry*, 15(1), 1–2.

This editorial reflects on the doctor–nurse relationship, and comments on how Leonard Stein's "doctor–nurse game" is changing in an environment where interprofessional collaboration is encouraged. The editorial touches on structural factors such as gender relations and professional power that will need to evolve for doctors and nurses to reach a higher level of mutual trust and a more fluid form of collaboration.

Reeves, S., Perrier, L., Goldman, J., Freeth, D., & Zwarenstein, M. (2013). Interprofessional education: Effects on professional practice and health care outcomes. *Cochrane Database of Systematic Reviews*, Issue 3.

This updated Cochrane review assesses the effectiveness of IPE interventions. Nine new studies were added to six existing studies (from the earlier 2008 update) for a total of fifteen studies included in the analysis. Although IPE was found to produce positive outcomes in some settings, the authors noted that the sample size was too small and heterogeneous to draw generalizable inferences. Recommendations are made regarding future areas of research.

Reeves, S., Russell, A., Zwarenstein, M., Kenaszchuk, C., Gotlib Conn, L., Doran, D. ... Strauss, S. (2007). Structuring communication relationships for interprofessional teamwork (SCRIPT): A Canadian initiative aimed at improving patient-centred care. *Journal of Interprofessional Care, 21*(1), 111–14.

This paper discusses the merits of a project based at the University of Toronto that aims to improve interprofessional development across three distinct clinical settings: general internal medicine, primary care, and rehabilitation and continuing care. The study employs a mixed-methods cluster randomized controlled trial incorporating twenty clinical teaching teams. Findings indicate that a significant portion of interprofessional interaction lacks key components of collaborative education.

Reeves, S., & Sully, P. (2007). Interprofessional education for practitioners working with the survivors of violence: Exploring early and longer-term outcomes on practice. *Journal of Interprofessional Care, 21*(4), 401–12.

An interprofessional course aimed to improve the care of patients who are survivors of violence is evaluated. An interpretivist framework is used to collect data through focus group interviews and individual follow-up interviews. Findings show that the course had a number of early effects on the participants' knowledge of working collaboratively with the survivors of violence.

Reeves, S., Tassone, M., Parker, K., Wagner, S.J., & Simmons, B. (2012). Interprofessional education: An overview of key developments in the past three decades. *Journal of Prevention Assessment and Rehabilitation, 41*(3), 233.

A narrative review of the salient IPE literature is conducted in relation to the field's development over the past thirty years. The results are discussed in relation to four categories: the emergence of IPE, learning and teaching approaches, an evidence base for IPE, and organizational elements. Conclusions for the future development of the field as well as potential implications are outlined.

Reeves, S., Zwarenstein, M., Goldman, J., Barr, H., Freeth, D., Koppel, I., & Hammick, M. (2010). The effectiveness of interprofessional education: Key findings from a new systematic review. *Journal of Interprofessional Care, 24*(3), 230–41.

After completing a second Cochrane review, the authors assess the six studies that meet the qualification requirements. The findings from this review suggest that although there are still many indications that IPE has a positive impact on patient care, more studies that employ both quantitative and qualitative methods need to be conducted to provide comprehensive insights into the effects of IPE.

Rice, K., Zwarenstein, M., Gotlib Conn, L., Kenaszchuk, C., Russell, A., & Reeves, S. (2010). An intervention to improve interprofessional collaboration and communications: A comparative qualitative study. *Journal of Interprofessional Care,* 24(4), 350–61.

An interprofessional intervention designed to help improve communication as well as collaboration between different professions in Canadian general internal medicine wards was examined using qualitative methods. The methods included ninety hours of ethnographic observation as well as interviews and documentary data. Findings suggested that the intended changes in communication and collaboration from the intervention were not successful.

Robichaud, P., Saari, M., Burnham, E., Omar, S., Wray, R.D., Baker, G.R., & Matlow, A.G. (2012). The value of a quality improvement project in promoting interprofessional collaboration. *Journal of Interprofessional Care,* 26(2), 158–60.

The study aims to show the possibility of utilizing quality improvement education to help promote interprofessional collaboration. The study considered self-reflections and the results of a focus group completed by twelve participants. The data analysis showed a greater understanding of interprofessionalism from the participants.

Rose, L. (2011). Interprofessional collaboration in the ICU: How to define? *Nursing in Critical Care,* 16(1), 5–10.

The author discusses the determining factors and the complexities surrounding interprofessional collaboration, as well as the evidence of positive patient outcomes resulting from interprofessional collaboration in the ICU. Interventions designed to foster a stronger interprofessional team are considered along with the necessary adjustments for the continued improvement of interprofessional teamwork in the ICU.

Rosenfield, D., Oandasan, I., & Reeves, S. (2011). Perceptions versus reality: A qualitative study of students' expectations and experiences of interprofessional education. *Medical Education,* 45(5), 471–7.

This study uses focus groups, over the span of two years, to determine the students' perception of large-scale interprofessional initiatives conducted during their first year of studies. The results reveal that although the students are interested in IPE, the large-scale events posed many challenges to the students' initial engagement with interprofessional concepts, teamwork, and collaboration.

Rosenfield, D., Oandasan, I., & Reeves, S. (2009). A participatory approach to interprofessional education research: Students researching with their peers. *Journal of Interprofessional Care,* 23(6), 676–8.

This study aims to evaluate students' perceptions of IPE initiatives at their university. Findings indicated medical students were weary of "contrived" interprofessional scenarios and would rather learn from shadowing/direct observation.

Russell, L., Nyhof, J., Abosh, B., & Robinson, S. (2006). An exploratory analysis of an interprofessional learning environment in two hospital clinical teaching units. *Journal of Interprofessional Care, 20*(1), 29–39.

This mixed-methods study explored different professionals' views of an interprofessional learning environment. Results highlight that students had little understanding of the nature of collaborative practice, and they learned attitudes and practices through tacit observation of staff behaviours.

Shahrokhi, S., Kunaal, J., & Jeschke, M.G. (2012). Three components of education in burn care: Surgical education, inter-professional education, and mentorship. *Burns, 28*(6), 783–9.

The authors discuss how different elements of training—including surgical education, interprofessional education, and mentorship—have been utilized in burn care education. Future directions regarding student learning in the field of burn care are also mentioned.

Sharma, B., Mishra, A., Aggarwal, R. & Grantcharov, T.P. (2011). Non-technical skills assessment in surgery. *Surgical Oncology, 20*(3), 169–77.

This review examines the importance of nontechnical skills in surgical oncology, including communication, teamwork, and decision making. Eleven articles are summarized and highlight the validity, reliability, and feasibility of three specific tools that have been used to evaluate nontechnical surgical skills. Recommendations are made for the inclusion of these tools, as well as other nontechnical rating scales, in surgical curriculum.

Simmons, B., Egan-Lee, E., Wagner, S., Esdaile, M., Baker, L., & Reeves, S. (2011). Assessment of interprofessional learning: The design of an interprofessional objective structured clinical examination (iOSCE) approach. *Journal of Interprofessional Care, 25*(1), 73–4.

This short report comments on the development of the iOSCE, the interprofessional OSCE. The authors describe the methods utilized to gain participation from all ten of the health professions at the University of Toronto, the topics and themes selected for potential clinical scenarios, and the iterative process in place to ensure the creation of a valid product.

Simmons, B., Oandasan, I., Soklaradis, S., Esdaile, M., Barker, K., Kwan, D. ...Wagner, S. (2011). Evaluating the effectiveness of an interprofessional education faculty development course: The transfer of interprofessional learning to the academic and clinical practice setting. *Journal of Interprofessional Care, 25*(2), 156–7.

This article evaluates the impact of a five-day certificate course, offered at the Centre for Interprofessional Education, which aims to develop the knowledge of IPE in faculty and clinicians working in academic and clinical settings. Participants' reflective reports revealed self-reported behavioural changes and intent to change as well as positive perceptions of the importance of IPE/IPC for collaborative patient-centered care.

Simmons, B., & Wagner, S. (2009). Assessment of continuing interprofessional education: Lessons learned. *Journal of Continuing Education in the Health Professions, 29*(3), 168–71.

This article explores key issues related to the assessment of continuing interprofessional education. The authors reflect on approaches to designing and integrating IPE into university curriculum, and propose the use of an assessment blueprint.

Sinclair, L.B., Lingard, L., & Mohabeer, R.N. (2009). What's so great about rehabilitation teams? An ethnographic study of interprofessional collaboration in a rehabilitation unit. *Archives of Physical Medicine and Rehabilitation, 90*(7), 1196–1201.

This ethnographic study explores team structures, relationships, and organizational culture as it relates to interprofessional collaboration in a rehabilitation setting. The authors describe recurrent examples of interprofessional collaboration within two dominant themes: team culture and communication structures. The findings reveal a perspective about the daily work clinicians face when providing interprofessional care.

Stergiou-Kita, M., Dawson, D., & Rappolt, S. (2012). Interprofessional clinical practice guideline for vocational evaluation following traumatic brain injury: A systematic and evidence-based approach. *Journal of Occupational Rehabilitation, 22*(2), 166–81.

The authors describe the development of an interprofessional clinical practice guideline designed to assist clinicians in collaboratively making decisions regarding patient care. A number of recommendations are proposed regarding the evaluation and utilization of this tool.

Suter, E., Goldman, J., Martimianakis, T., Chatalalsign, C., DeMatteo, D., & Reeves, S. (2013). The use of systems and organizational theories in the interprofessional field: Findings from a scoping review. *Journal of Interprofessional Care, 27*(1), 57–64.

This paper summarizes findings from a broader scoping review

of theories in educational and organizational literature targeted toward the improvement of interprofessional education and practice. The authors offer new insight into theories that support the design and implementation of interprofessional education and practice initiatives.

Taggart, K. (2011). University of Toronto's interprofessional centre emphasizes health-care teamwork. *Medical Post, 47*(1), 36–37.

Taggart describes the programs made available by the University of Toronto's interprofessional centre, which emphasize health care teamwork across eleven health science programs. Some of the unique interprofessional initiatives embedded within a health care student's education are discussed as well optional interprofessional clinical placements.

Van Soeren, M., Baker, L., Egan–Lee, E., MacMillan, K., Devlin-Cop, S., & Reeves, S. (2011). Simulated interprofessional education: An analysis of teaching and learning processes. *Journal of Interprofesional Care, 25*(6), 434–40.

This exploratory study provides insight into the learning processes embedded within simulated learning activities through the use of qualitative methods. The 265 participants were composed of clinicians, students, and facilitators. The analysis of video-recorded role-plays and debriefing sessions revealed five key themes

that point to the importance of deliberate and skilled facilitation.

Van Soeren, M., Hurlock–Chorostecki, C., & Reeves, S. (2011). The role of nurse practitioners in hospital settings: Implications for interprofessional practice. *Journal of Interprofessional Care, 25*(4), 245–51.

The study aims to determine how the role of the nurse practitioner functions within interprofessional health care teams. A mixed-methods approach including on-site tracking and observation, self-recorded logs, and focus group interviews was utilized. Findings suggest that the scope of care of nurse practitioners is encouraging more interprofessional communication.

Verman, S., Medves, J., Paterson, M., & Patteson, A. (2006). Demonstrating interprofessional education using a workshop model. *Journal of Interprofessional Care, 20*(6), 679–81.

This article describes the development and evaluation of an interprofessional workshop for faculty. Results from the post-workshop survey indicate that participants underwent a change in knowledge and perceptions regarding IPE.

Verma, S., Paterson, M., & Medves, J. (2006). Core competencies for health care professionals: What medicine, nursing, occupational therapy and physiotherapy share. *Journal of Allied Health, 35*(2), 109–15.

This paper describes the amalgamation of core competencies, identified across health professions, into a framework for IPE. The model was created as a basis for curriculum design. The authors highlight the relevance of cross-disciplinary competency teaching and provide the groundwork for performance standards in interprofessional learning.

Waters I., Barker, K., & Kwan, D. (2005). Interprofessional care training program pilot project. *Journal of Interprofessional Care, 19*(2), 174–5.

This short report provides a summary of a proposed pilot qualitative study, the interprofessional care training program. The purpose of the study is to explore senior health care learners' experiences in an interprofessional patient care clinic.

Waterston, R. (2011). Interaction in online interprofessional education case discussions. *Journal of Interprofessional Care, 25*(4), 272–9.

This study investigates the online interaction within an IP curriculum unit, "Pain Week," at the University of Toronto. Nine of the eighty-one teams that completed the unit were selected for detailed review. Differences between the units

that gave positive feedback versus negative feedback were situated within a theoretical framework drawn from the contact theory, the community inquiry model, and the social independence theory.

Watt-Watson, J., Hunter, P., Pennefather, L., Librach, L., Raman-Wilms, M., Schreiber, J., ... Salter, M. (2004). An integrated undergraduate curriculum, based on International Association for the Study of Pain curricula, for six health Science Faculties. *Pain 110*(1-2), 140–8.

This theoretical article reviews different conceptual models to address doctor barriers to collaboration and suggests ways to increase the effectiveness of IPE programs. The current nature of pain education team function in the health care system is examined as well as the aspects of socialization that may hinder doctor engagement in the aims of IPE.

Whitehead, C. (2007). The doctor dilemma in interprofessional education and care: How and why will physicians collaborate? *Medical Education, 41*(10), 1010–16.

This discussion paper provides an overview of physician barriers to collaboration. Aspects of medical education and socialization are explored. The author offers suggestions to increase the impact of IPE programs, particularly as it relates to the acknowledgment of power differentials and varying degrees of professional authority.

Whyte, S., Lingard, L., Espin, S., Baker, G.R., Bohnen, J., Orser, B.A. ... Regehr, G. (2008). Paradoxical effects of interprofessional briefings on OR team performance. *Cognition, Technology & Work, 10*(4), 287–94.

Building on the work of Lingard et al. (2005), this qualitative study explores the effects of structured interprofessional communications in the operating room setting. The authors identify five paradoxical findings and analyze them in relation to educational, functional, structural, and cultural factors.

Yoon, M.N., & Steele, C.M. (2012). Health care professionals' perspectives on oral care for long-term care residents: Nursing staff, speech-language pathologists and dental hygienists. *Gerodontology, 29*(2), 525–35.

This study explores various health professions' perspectives regarding oral health in the long-term care setting. Data from the focus groups suggests that oral health maintenance is typically considered a nursing staff role, while advocacy and education are assumed by speech-language pathologists and dental hygienists. Suggestions are made regarding the value of collaboration within multidisciplinary teams to promote oral health.

Zwarenstein, M., Bryant, W., & Reeves, S. (2003). In-service interprofessional education improves inpatient care and patient satisfaction. *Journal of Interprofessional Care, 17*(4), 401–2.

This research report discusses the outcome of the Level of Care Intervention Study project, which grew out of concern that a South African teaching hospital was providing "routinized care" not tailored to patient needs. The interprofessional training intervention succeeded in improving communication among the medical staff, in improving overall patient satisfaction, and in lowering pharmaceutical and laboratory costs.

Zwarenstein, M., Goldman, J., & Reeves, S. (2009). Interprofessional collaboration: Effects of practice-based interventions on professional practice and healthcare outcomes. *Cochrane Database of Systematic Reviews*, Issue 3.

This Cochrane review assesses the impact of practice-based interventions on interprofessional collaboration. Five studies met the inclusion criteria; however, a meta-analysis of the study outcomes was not possible, given their heterogeneity and small sample size. Recommendations are made regarding future research in the field of interprofessional collaboration.

Zwarenstein, M., & Reeves, S. (2006). Knowledge translation and interprofessional collaboration: Where the rubber of evidence-based care hits the road of teamwork. *Journal of Continuing Education in the Health Professions, 26*(1), 46–54.

The authors describe a randomized trial, funded by Health Canada, where quantitative and

qualitative data is collected in twenty Toronto internal medicine units. The impact of interprofessional education and collaboration interventions on health care practices, patient outcomes, and interprofessional relationships are examined.

Zwarenstein, M., Reeves, S., & Perrier, L. (2005). Effectiveness of pre-licensure interprofessional education and post-licensure collaborative interventions. *Journal of Interprofessional Care, 19*(Suppl. 1), 148–65.

This article summarizes empirical evidence regarding the impact of both pre-licensure and post-licensure interventions on the delivery of care. The authors conclude that there is a growing body of evidence regarding the effectiveness of post-licensure interventions; however, more work is needed regarding pre-licensure activities.

Zwarenstein, M., Reeves, S., Russell, A., Kenaszchuk, C., Gotlib Conn, L., Miller, K.L., ... Thorpe, K.E. (2007). Structuring communication relationships for interprofessional teamwork (SCRIPT): A cluster randomized controlled trial. *Trial, 18*(8), 23.

This article outlines the objectives and methods of an ongoing multi-center, mixed-methods randomized controlled trial. The primary aim of the study is to evaluate the effects of a hospital-based communication protocol on various outcomes related to interprofessional collaboration and patient care.